For Frank,
my partner in everything.

(FH)

THE GIANT
OTTER

GIANTS OF THE AMAZON

Jessica Groenendijk

WHITE OWL
AN IMPRINT OF PEN & SWORD BOOKS LTD.
YORKSHIRE – PHILADELPHIA

First published in Great Britain in 2019 by
Pen and Sword WHITE OWL
An imprint of
Pen & Sword Books Ltd
Yorkshire - Philadelphia

ISBN 978 1 52671 174 8

Typeset in 11/14 pts Palatino
by Aura Technology and Software Services, India

Printed and bound in India by Replika Press Pvt. Ltd.

Pen & Sword Books Ltd incorporates the Imprints of Pen & Sword Books Archaeology,
Atlas, Aviation, Battleground, Discovery, Family History, History, Maritime, Military,
Naval, Politics, Railways, Select, Transport, True Crime, Fiction, Frontline Books, Leo
Cooper, Praetorian Press, Seaforth Publishing, Wharncliffe and White Owl.

For a complete list of Pen & Sword titles please contact

PEN & SWORD BOOKS LIMITED
47 Church Street, Barnsley, South Yorkshire, S70 2AS, England
E-mail: enquiries@pen-and-sword.co.uk
Website: www.pen-and-sword.co.uk

or

PEN AND SWORD BOOKS
1950 Lawrence Rd, Havertown, PA 19083, USA
E-mail: Uspen-and-sword@casematepublishers.com
Website: www.penandswordbooks.com

Contents

Acknowledgements

FOR A LIFE WITH GIANT OTTERS

Many, many people have made my involvement with giant otters over the past two decades, and hence the writing of this book, possible. I am indebted to them all. But there are those who I would like to single out to express my deepest gratitude:

Wouter Veening (Institute for Environmental Security) and Hemmo Muntingh (International Fund for Animal Welfare) for introducing giant otters into my life. This is all your fault.

Dr. Christof Schenck, Dr. Elke Staib, and the Frankfurt Zoological Society, for giving me the chance to live my dream, for sharing their data unreservedly, and for supporting our work.

Dr. Nicole Duplaix and the IUCN/SSC Otter Specialist Group, especially the Giant Otter Section, for making me feel a valued member of the giant otter research community.

Prof. David Macdonald, Dr. Paul Johnson, Dr. Chris Newman, and Dr. Lauren Harrington, (Wildlife Conservation Research Unit, University of Oxford), for helping me publish our findings. I couldn't have done it without you.

The Peruvian Service for Natural Protected Areas (SERNANP) and our field assistants Dario Cruz, Zacarias Flores, Benjamin Cruz, Armando Cruz, and Wilfredo Valles, for making our fieldwork possible and for ensuring that each of our many trips to the rivers and lakes of Madre de Dios was a unique and rewarding experience.

Frank Hajek, for accompanying me throughout this journey.

And lastly, the giant otters of Madre de Dios, for enriching my life immeasurably.

FOR THIS BOOK

I am extremely grateful to Frank Hajek, Dr. Nicole Duplaix, Walter Wust, João Marcos Rosa, Dr. Ron Swaisgood, Dr. Fernando Trujillo, André Bärtschi, Carlos Arévalo, and Dr. Adi Barocas for so generously sharing their photos to illustrate the text.

Also to Dr. Christof Schenck, Director of the Frankfurt Zoological Society, for contributing his thoughts on why giant otters are so large; Dr. Helen Bateman of the Center for Conservation and Research of Endangered Wildlife (CREW) at the

(FH)

Cincinnati Zoo, for helping me make sense of giant otter reproductive biology; and Ignacio Jiménez, Conservation Coordinator of the Conservation Land Trust, for information on the giant otter reintroduction project in Argentina.

To my family – Frank, and our children, Saba and Luca – for being so understanding and supportive while I buried myself in this book.

And thank you, Jonathan Wright, Janet Brookes, and the wonderful, patient staff at Pen & Sword Ltd., for giving me this opportunity to share my passion for giant otters.

Foreword

I am not a giant otter expert, but fell in love at first sight with this iconic and charismatic species of the Amazon. I recall drinking my morning coffee while looking out over the still waters of the oxbow lake at the Cocha Cashu Biological Station in the Peruvian Amazon. My peaceful moment was suddenly interrupted by a great commotion, an effervescence of rolling water, then one head, and another emerged above the water. From the mouth of one dangled a large, wriggling fish and the otter made quick work of it. At first, in the midst of the excitement, they didn't seem to notice me, but soon, joined by two younger otters, all eyes turned to me. I'm no anthropomorphist, but they seemed earnest and quizzical. I was smitten. Since that experience I have enjoyed many more, from the shore or in a small canoe, and I am unfailingly impressed and endeared with these active, rambunctious, and intelligent animals.

I am a conservation biologist with a focus on species. While my interest in animals extends far beyond the large and charismatic ones, I soon realised the giant otter was deserving of my attention. Fortunately, the Amazon does not yet face the extinction crisis we see in other parts of the world, like Asia, the Pacific islands, or southern California — places where I routinely apply my craft in the service of at-risk species — but the giant otter was once almost lost to us. Highly prized for its pelt, it was hunted nearly to extinction before the fur trade was banned and the otter began to make a comeback. Now, that recovery is being undermined by a host of new, emerging threats we do not fully understand. It's difficult to imagine that there are not more

(FH)

otter biologists than there are otters themselves, given their charm, but it seems clear there are some large research gaps out there that could impede recovery of the species.

In a nutshell this is how I came to be involved in giant otter research and conservation. At my organisation, San Diego Zoo Global, we are committed to using the best science to solve conservation problems for individual species. We are also proud to be managing the Cocha Cashu Biological Station deep in Manu National Park, one of the last strongholds of the giant otter and other at-risk Amazonian species. 'Cashu,' as we call it, has, as one of its missions, the goal of using the forests and lakes around the station as a sort of ultimate control site for scientific research of nature as it should be. Data collected at Cashu can serve as an important baseline, guiding conservation and restoration elsewhere. The resident family of giant otters is included in a larger study we embarked upon in 2017 that investigates gold mining, fishing, and other anthropogenic threats. We are comparing how these otters and others living under the protective umbrella of Manu National Park are faring compared with those impacted by human activities and, potentially, mercury contamination from gold mining. This will allow us to tease out the consequences of these activities on otter health, survival, and reproduction, ultimately affecting their ability to persist into the future. Other emerging threats, such as pathogens from the increasing presence of domestic animals in and around the protected areas of the Amazon, are an additional cause for concern that should be explored.

All too often our expertise is called into play after a species has suffered a precipitous decline, one that may even warrant a captive breeding programme as an assurance population while we endeavour to turn things around on the ground in the species' range. At other times there is still a sufficient population remaining in the wild but it has been extirpated from such a large area that we must use translocation as a tool for re-establishing or supplementing wild populations. These kinds of intensive interventions are a sad statement on the state of affairs for wildlife. The giant otter was almost brought to this point in the extinction vortex, but fortunately the ban on the fur trade allowed for a natural and slow recovery. Now that this recovery is jeopardised, it is incumbent upon conservation scientists to get out in front of the emerging threats, study them, and help devise plans to mitigate them.

Let's not let the giant otter become the next California condor or Arabian oryx in need of rescue from extinction's door. Instead, let's put our heads together and come up with some workable solutions for this icon of the Amazon today. In my old age, when I visit the Amazon on more feeble legs, I hope I can still enjoy a good coffee in the company of these magnificent creatures.

Dr. Ron Swaisgood, Director, Recovery Ecology
Institute for Conservation Research, San Diego Zoo Global
4 February 2019

Presentation

Groups of ecotourists watch a noisy family of giant otters swim across the lake in Manu National Park, Peru. They take photographs, laugh, and love the experience. They have probably travelled from far away just to share a precious moment with these charismatic animals. I wonder if they know just how close the giant otter came to extinction.

For forty years, hunters shot giant otters on sight for their velvety soft fur. They tracked them up every river, every forest creek until they were gone. Only remote areas remained pristine. Suriname and Guyana were among the lucky few countries where giant otters were unmolested. In 1975, the giant otter was proclaimed: 'One of the ten most endangered carnivores on earth.' Clearly, this was an emergency and it goaded me into action. We knew virtually nothing about this species and we had no idea what actions to take to save it. I had watched otters in zoos, comparing the

(ND)

behaviours of six different otter species but had not spent much time studying them in the wild. Undaunted, I set off for Suriname and spent the next two years exploring its rivers and getting to know the giant otter.

Giant otters travel in groups, patrolling their territories during the day, and raise a noisy alarm whenever another otter family, or an eager researcher, shows up. A group approached my boat to investigate the newcomer. No wonder it had been so easy for hunters to shoot them. After a few months, one family accepted my presence and I could watch them all day as they fished and rested on the bank. What a joy, what a privilege.

Now, forty years later, there is good news and bad news for the giant otter. Thanks to the 1973 CITES convention that bans all trade in endangered species, giant otters made a comeback, in the nick of time, in most of their 12 range countries. In some areas, like the Pantanal in Brazil and protected areas in Peru, these otters are now the darlings of ecotourists, but serious threats remain elsewhere.

One threat is potentially deadly but often invisible. The soaring price of gold has created a frantic gold rush in South America and this time not even the once pristine Guianas have been spared. Gold prospectors invade the most remote areas, protected parks, indigenous homelands. With their chainsaws, pumps, mercury, and a total disregard for the forest, they devastate creeks and rivers, leaving behind torrents of poisoned mud that slowly flow hundreds of kilometres to the sea. Mercury is a particularly toxic heavy metal, for fish-eating animals and humans alike, that accumulates in body tissues. People who live along these contaminated waters and depend on fish for their survival are particularly vulnerable to this slow death by poisoning.

All is not lost, however. We can protect giant otters by creating more protected areas in their habitats. We can put pressure on governments to discourage illegal gold miners and protect rivers, the livelihood of indigenous fishing communities. Public opinion is a strong motivator for change and we need change if we are to have a healthy ecosystem to enjoy for decades to come.

My friend, Jessica Groenendijk, has written an amazing book about our favourite species. It has been an honour and joy for both of us to get to know the giant otter that shares our planet. Every day we learn a new detail about their behaviour or biology that fascinates us. It is our love of otters over many decades that gives us the courage to do all we can to make sure these amazing animals never disappear.

Dr. Nicole Duplaix
Chair, IUCN/SSC Otter Specialist Group
4 February 2019

(JMR)

'He was boneless, mercurial, sinuous, wonderful... he was
an otter in his own element and the most beautiful thing
in nature I had ever seen.'

Gavin Maxwell, *Ring of Bright Water*
First published in Great Britain by Longmans Green 1960
First published in the United States of America by E. P. Dutton & Co. Inc., 1961

Author's Note

have been involved with giant otters, in one way or another, since 1998. That, I now realise, covers two decades, almost half my life.

It all started with a literature study commissioned by the International Fund for Animal Welfare (IFAW). Actually, it started before that, with a Geographical Society sponsored expedition to the Las Piedras River in south-eastern Peru. I saw giant otters in the wild for the first time and mentioned the experience to my colleagues; I was then working at the Netherlands Committee for IUCN (International Union for Conservation of Nature) in Amsterdam. Shortly after, the Director of IFAW Europe, Hemmo Muntingh, was looking for someone to undertake the literature study, with a focus on the Guiana Shield region, and his close friend and my boss, Wouter Veening, suggested that he ask me. My investigations into the world of giant otters and their conservation took me to Trebon, Czech Republic, where I participated in my first

(JG)

International Otter Colloquium, organised by the IUCN Otter Specialist group. And that eventually led to my becoming the coordinator, in 1999, of a long term giant otter research and conservation field project in south-eastern Peru, run by the Frankfurt Zoological Society.

Seven years later, in 2006, I co-authored a book, together with my husband Frank Hajek, entitled *Giants of the Madre de Dios*, on giant otters and their conservation in Peru. The level of knowledge about the behaviour and ecology of this apex predator has increased substantially since then, so this book is intended to serve both as a revised and updated edition of the first publication, as well as a more complete review of what is known about the species throughout its distribution range.

Much as I would have liked to include even the smallest detail of giant otter biology, ecology, and behaviour, I have restricted myself to what I consider the most important or intriguing aspects. Also, please note that some photos shown on the following pages are of otters under rehabilitation although the majority are of wild individuals. Lastly, to avoid cluttering the text with numerous citations, and because this is not intended to be an academic paper, I have opted to list all references and articles for further reading at the end of the book. I hope the many authors whose excellent published work has nourished this text will understand.

Jessica Groenendijk
4 February 2019

Introduction

There are numerous reasons why both scientists and non-scientists are fascinated by the charismatic giant otter. Confined to rainforests and freshwater wetlands in South America, this top carnivore has a complex social life, living in close-knit groups, hunting fish communally, and with older offspring helping to care for the youngest members. A giant otter family has much in common with its human counterpart, which is why observing them over many years has something of a soap opera about it. There's sibling rivalry and play, unity in the face of a threat, shared responsibilities including babysitting and feeding of the cubs, and, finally, mature offspring leaving home and starting families of their own.

The giant otter is a carnivorous mammal that belongs to the Lutrinae subfamily, together with 12 other species of otter, and to the family Mustelidae, which also includes the weasels, badgers, martins, mink, polecats, and wolverines. In giant

(FH)

otter literature, the first description of the species (*Pteronura brasiliensis*) is attributed to a German geographer, mathematician, and naturalist, Professor Eberhard August Wilhelm von Zimmerman, in 1780. Brief but florid, and often inaccurate or exaggerated observations recorded by early Amazon explorers over the next two centuries were succeeded during the 1960s and '70s by more detailed publications on the diet and reproductive behaviour of captive animals.

Though wild populations of giant otters may have featured little in academic papers up to this point, on the ground in much of South America, dramatic developments were bringing this once abundant and widely distributed species to its knees. During the 1940s, '50s and '60s, giant otters became the target of the international commercial pelt trade. Skins were sold by the tens of thousands every year to luxury markets in Europe, US, and Japan, and in 1972 the IUCN Species Survival Commission (IUCN/SSC) declared the giant otter one of the ten most threatened mammals, stating that research was urgently required to determine its conservation needs.

Trade bans came into effect in most range countries between the late 1960s and mid-1970s but despite legal protection the situation was such that in March 1977 and again in 1980, the IUCN/SSC Otter Specialist Group designated the giant otter as their top priority for conservation. In 1980, Nicole Duplaix published the results of her pioneering field study into the ecology and behaviour of wild giant otters, carried out over a period of 20 months in Suriname. This was followed soon after by Liz Laidler's 15 month doctoral study near Georgetown, Guyana; three separate field projects at Cocha Cashu, in Peru's Manu National Park, led by Beatriz Torres, Brigitte Fugger, and Martha Brecht-Munn; a 1,600 km river population survey in El Tuparro National Park, Colombia, by Thomas Defler; and Jorge Schweizer's extensive field observations in Brazil.

The 1990 IUCN Action Plan for Latin American Otters stated that: 'The giant otter's range has been greatly reduced and its diurnal, social habits, along with its size (and consequent pelt value) make it exceptionally vulnerable; the species is severely threatened...' and continued to specify that, for Peru, a conservation priority was to 'Monitor closely the main identified populations, particularly the giant otters of Manu National Park...'. Thus, in late 1990, the Frankfurt Zoological Society initiated what is now the world's longest running giant otter population monitoring and conservation programme, in the Madre de Dios region of south-eastern Peru (see map overleaf). In its early years, German biologists Christof Schenck and Elke Staib both contributed doctorate dissertations to the existing body of knowledge. My own involvement in this program began in 1999 when Frank and I succeeded Christof and Elke as its coordinators. In 2006 Frank and I moved to Zambia to work with black rhinos, so it is our joint findings over the first 16 years of this program that I refer to repeatedly in this book.

Our two main study areas were the oxbow lakes and lower reaches of the Manu River (150 to 200 metres wide) in Manu National Park, and the Palma Real River and its main tributary the Patuyacu River (both 20 to 50 metres in width) in the Tambopata National Reserve, on the border of Bahuaja Sonene National Park. Both the Palma Real and the Manu are whitewater tributaries of the mighty Madre de Dios River, but the Palma Real is much smaller and lacks the oxbow lakes that characterise the Manu floodplain and are favoured by the giant otter. We conducted annual giant otter population surveys on both river systems in order to better understand their demography and conservation status.

Meanwhile, numerous other studies were initiated in Colombia, Bolivia, Ecuador, French Guiana, Paraguay, and in various parts of Brazil, including the Balbina

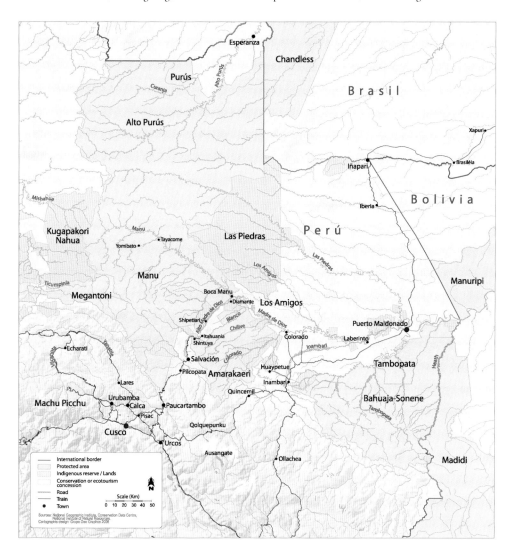

hydroelectric reservoir, the Pantanal, and the Xixuaú Reserve, to name but a few. As a result of the increased interest in and concern for the species, the giant otter is no longer an obscure, little known animal, sought after only for its pelt. Within the space of four decades it has become a much-loved ambassador for tropical wetland ecosystems, the star of numerous articles and nature documentaries, and an outstanding model for research into important questions of evolutionary, behavioural, and conservation biology.

THE AMAZON

It seems only fitting that the world's largest otter should make a region of superlatives its home. Named after the immense river that dominates it, the Amazon encompasses the most extensive remaining tropical rainforest in the world and shelters at least one tenth of the planet's known biodiversity. The basin covers some 40% of the South American continent and includes parts of eight countries: Bolivia, Brazil, Colombia, Ecuador, Guyana, Peru, Suriname, and Venezuela, as well as French Guiana, a department of France. 'If there is any place on Earth still deserving of the term 'wilderness' it is surely the Amazon,' writes Dr. Lisa Davenport in her 2008 giant otter doctorate dissertation. That may well be true but the neighbouring Pantanal, to the south, comes close: at 70,000 square miles it is the world's largest tropical wetland and boasts the highest wildlife concentration on the continent, as well as important populations of the giant otter. And then there is the Orinoco River basin, covering

(WW)

some 880,000 km², including most of Venezuela and eastern Colombia, and home to over 1,000 species of fish as well as the giant otter. Thus, for the sake of convenience, I am taking the liberty of using the word 'Amazon' in the sub title of this book as an all-encompassing name for the entire region currently inhabited by the species in South America.

THE GIANT OTTER

Giant otters are exceptionally well adapted to life in rivers, lakes and swamps of the tropical lowlands of South America. Known as *lobo de rio* or 'river wolf' in Peru, it is both the largest (at between one and a half to almost two metres in length, they are as long as a person is tall) and arguably the most social of the world's 13 otter species. Each individual has a distinctive pale throat pattern, as unique as a fingerprint, by which it can be identified, thereby greatly facilitating field research. Giant otters are apex carnivores of the rainforest and have little to fear... except man.

Though the species is currently protected both by national legislation in all range countries as well as by the Convention on International Trade in Endangered Species of Wild Flora and Fauna (CITES), its distribution has been greatly reduced and is now discontinuous, with only small, isolated populations remaining. While some of these are stable and others are even increasing, the species remains threatened throughout its distribution range: it is officially categorised in national Red Lists as Vulnerable in Brazil, Endangered or Critically Endangered in eight other countries, and Extinct in Uruguay. Giant otters face severe pressures exerted by widespread and increasing human colonisation, as well as intensive exploitation of natural resources by man, leading to the contamination and destruction of formerly pristine rainforest and wetland systems.

In the first chapter of this book we meet the giant otter; I describe its general appearance and most striking features and provide an overview of its basic ecology, behaviour, habitat, and geographical distribution. Having set the scene and introduced the main character, so to speak, we delve deeper in Chapter Two as it guides us through a day in the life of a giant otter family. In Chapter Three we accompany a disperser during the trials and tribulations of a year spent looking for a mate and a territory of its own. Chapter Four summarises past and current threats to the survival of the species. Lastly,

The giant otter is a top carnivore of the wetlands of Madre de Dios. The species is rare in much of its former range and extinct in Argentina and Uruguay. (ND)

in Chapter Five, I describe a variety of conservation actions that have benefited the otters over the last decades and propose additional steps we can take to further conservation of the species. The focus in this final chapter is largely on personal experiences and observations in south-eastern Peru, not because other countries have not undertaken conservation measures to protect the giant otter — they have — but because by using Peru as a case study I can go into rather more detail. Much of what has been, and is being achieved in Peru, can be extrapolated to other parts of the giant otter's distribution range.

In Chapters Two and Three, I have ventured to include short descriptions in italics of typical behaviour, scenery, and other wildlife from the giant otter's perspective as I picture it to be. I am aware of the scientist's mistrust of anthropomorphism, yet I firmly believe that animals other than ourselves experience emotions and sensations in ways that are both similar and different to ours, and that empathy and imagination only serve to increase our understanding of their worlds, while enriching our own.

Finally, I have included a personal anecdote at the end of each chapter in the hope of sharing with you the wonder, and difficulties, of life following the giants of the Amazon.

CHAPTER ONE

Meet the Giant Otter

*S*eptember 1998: We slowly make our way up a small tributary of the Madre de Dios River, surveying its banks for signs of the otters. We've been traveling for five days without sighting a single individual, although we spotted several fresh dens this morning and know they are around. Or have we somehow passed them? Have they noticed our progress upriver and neatly taken a shortcut overland to avoid us?

As we motor past a small beach just before a sharp bend in the river, someone points out a series of giant otter footprints at the water's edge. We stop to investigate. The tracks lead up to a marking site that has been so recently used, insects have not yet arrived at the scene. Circular sweep marks and bedraggled vegetation, leaves still wet, tell the story of how the otters have busily scent marked the beach. They can't be far so we decide to paddle upriver rather than use the motor.

Advancing laboriously against the current, we round the curve... and there they are. Suddenly, we find ourselves in the midst of a group of five giant otters. They surge towards us from all directions, periscoping – craning their heads and necks out of the water – and

(ND)

snorting repeatedly, clearly alarmed to have been approached so unexpectedly. We keep as low a profile as is possible in a twelve metre canoe, avoiding abrupt movements and saying little. Gradually, their focus seems to turn inwards: the otters begin milling about, as if confused. Without warning, one individual utters a harsh, wavering scream and the whole family lets loose a burst of sound. The volume at such close quarters is stunning and sends shivers down my spine. A sixth otter who must have been hunting by himself further upriver wails in response, swimming rapidly towards the family. Once reunited, they all head downriver, giving us a wide berth and looking back frequently before disappearing from view.

APPEARANCE

On encountering a giant otter for the first time, the feature that is likely to impress you most, as its name suggests, is its size. Known through much of its range as the 'water dog' or 'river wolf', it is one of South America's top carnivores. At 1.5 to 1.8 metres in total length, it is the largest of the world's 13 otter species although the sea otter (*Enhydra lutris*) is heavier, weighing as much as 42 kilograms compared to the river wolf's maximum of 34 kilos or so. Both sexes are 'giants' — in contrast to many other otter species where body size and weight differ significantly between the sexes, sexual dimorphism in giant otters is not pronounced.

This adult male giant otter is in superb condition. In the water below, on the left, is his cub. Note its smaller head and more pronounced ears. (ND)

Not unlike a seal in appearance, the giant otter is primarily terrestrial but, like the seal, has become exceptionally well adapted to the pursuit of prey in aquatic environments. When on land, it appears hunched and clumsy due to its elongated, low body, broad pelvis, and narrow shoulders. Nonetheless, it may travel considerable (though always the shortest possible) distances between water bodies, tending to use well-worn paths. The giant otter has short, stubby legs and large feet, with five long toes and thick webbing extending to their tips. Sharp, curved claws help it grip its prey and climb steep, slippery banks. The giant's long and supple body ends in a tail nearly half its body length, wing-shaped (hence the prefix *Ptero* in its scientific name),

An adult giant otter footprint is almost the size and shape of a human hand. The interdigital webbing is just visible in this set of tracks on damp clay. (FH)

These feet are made for grasping... and swimming. Fish rarely get away once in the grip of a giant otter. (FT)

thickly muscular at the base, and dorsoventrally flattened like a beaver's. On entering the water, the otter doggy-paddles. At high speed the undulating tail maintains momentum, while the feet are hardly used except to steer. When fishing, giant otters travel slowly, about one mile per hour, compared to an average of four miles per hour when swimming in a specific direction. When fully submerged, otters can move much faster, up to 10 miles per hour over short distances.

The body is covered with a pelt so fine it almost led to the river wolf's undoing. Velvety brown when dry and shiny dark chocolate when wet, it consists of a layer of

Having fine, dense, waterproof fur is a great thing for an otter, but it almost led to the giant's undoing. (FH)

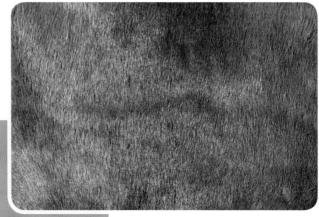

Without their unique throat markings, with which giant otters are identifiable from birth, the work of giant otter researchers would be a lot harder. (JG)

dense under-fur and a second layer of slightly longer (one centimetre), water-repellent guard hairs. An irregular pattern of pale markings on the chin, throat, and chest is unique to each individual from birth, ranging in appearance from a large, white bib to one or two tiny flecks. Rarely, a throat marking is entirely absent. It is the giant otter's distinctive white throat marking and its larger size which distinguishes it most readily from the similarly built and sympatric Neotropical otter (*Lontra longicaudis*).

The giant's comparatively small head is broad and somewhat flattened, with a blunt muzzle, powerful jaws, slightly domed forehead, and supported by a long, muscular neck. Large, dark eyes and a nose pad (or rhinarium) that is completely haired, unique in the Lutrinae, are positioned well to the top of the head so the otter can breathe and look around while the rest of its body remains submerged. Giants hunt primarily by sight and can alter the curvature of the lens to see better underwater, giving their eyes a somewhat opaque, bulging appearance. Above water, they are able to recognise family members and human observers at a distance of 50 metres.

The ears are small and rounded and, together with the nostrils, may be closed to prevent entry of water while diving. Numerous stiff but sensitive whiskers on the muzzle, brow, and temples help the otter detect movement and locate its prey in muddy water. Giant otters have a keen sense of smell over distances greater than 100 metres and hearing is acute, although sound location may be poor.

The river wolf has 36 teeth (incisors 3/3, canines 1/1, premolars 4/3, and molars 1/2), with the lower premolar occasionally absent. Its bite force has not been measured

A giant otter's head bristles with whiskers that come in handy when chasing fish or negotiating through murky water. (FH)

Giant otters have an extremely keen sense of smell. Here a dispersing otter sniffs at a log where a family has rested. (FH)

The river wolf is well equipped for a carnivorous diet. (ND)

but is sufficient to crack open fish skulls. Giant otters always eat their prey head first, and only large catfish are not eaten this way because of the size and hardness of their skulls. So, although a giant otter's bite force is probably significant, it will not be in the league of a jaguar's, and, unlike the jaguar, they are unable to break open a turtle shell.

When investigating something unfamiliar or the approach of an intruder, a giant otter will 'periscope', a term that accurately describes the manner in which it cranes its head and neck perpendicularly out of the water while remaining stationary by treading with all four feet.

SEXING

In the wild, it is only possible to determine the gender of individuals when they are observed out of the water, usually during resting and grooming sessions. Adult females with a litter will have an 'udder' and full teats while those who have nursed young have four permanently elongated teats (due to prolonged lactation). Adult males are readily distinguished by the obvious presence of testes (the male's scrotum does not become clearly evident until he is at least one year old): we noticed these sometimes become enlarged, perhaps indicating seasonal testicular activity.

This photo of a male giant otter basking on a log, utterly relaxed, was taken from a tree on the shore. (FH)

The breeding female is easily recognised by her four greatly elongated teats. There is no marked difference in body size between males and females. (FH)

However, gender is more difficult to determine in adult females that have not lactated, or in cubs and juveniles of both sexes.

In 2002, we stumbled upon a simple and effective method of sexing giant otters while they use a latrine. Otters often defecate and urinate simultaneously, with scats having a semi liquid consistency. We found that males can be told apart from females by the greater distance between the sources of the urine and faecal streams, that is, the genital and anal openings. When viewed broadside on, the male's urine stream has its source between the hind legs and the orientation of the stream is to the rear at a 45-60 degree angle. In females, the source of urine is close to the base of the tail and the stream projects downwards. In both males and females, the scat drops directly below the anus at the base of the tail. Hence, in males, the two streams often bisect each other with the urine stream landing beyond the scats, while in females they are parallel.

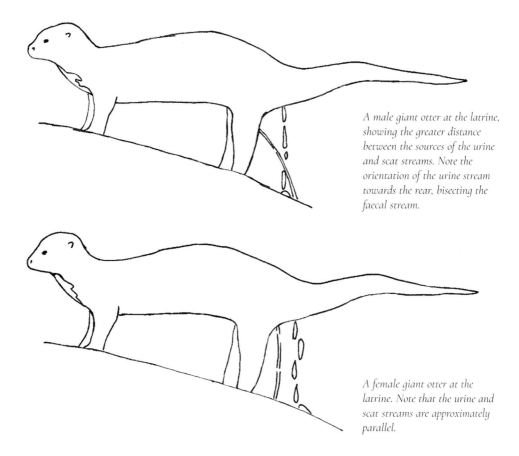

A male giant otter at the latrine, showing the greater distance between the sources of the urine and scat streams. Note the orientation of the urine stream towards the rear, bisecting the faecal stream.

A female giant otter at the latrine. Note that the urine and scat streams are approximately parallel.

FAMILY COHESION

The members of a giant otter family, and especially the breeding pair, are almost always together, often in physical contact, for example while grooming, playing, and resting, or in close proximity, usually within sight of each other. When cubs lag behind, older members soon turn back to chivvy them along, and when the breeding female initiates an activity or changes direction, the other group members usually follow suit. Only individuals that are approaching sexual maturity may begin to absent themselves from the group for several hours or a day, before becoming fully independent.

A striking illustration of a family's cohesiveness was documented in Manu, when group members were observed coming to the aid of an elderly female member that had ceased to reproduce and struggled to keep up. On three occasions, after the otters had been engaged in high speed chases in pursuit of fish, her family helped her to rejoin the group. They also repeatedly shared their catches with her when she begged, assistance that is normally offered only to youngsters.

Why provide such support to an aged individual who has outlived her capacity to breed? It could be that group members respond instinctively to behaviour normally

Strong bonds unite the members of a giant otter family. (ABO)

associated with cubs. But the matriarch would also have accumulated valuable knowledge of the territory during her long tenure, of spatial and temporal location and variation of fish resources, and where to best establish dens and campsites. And is it too much to suppose that tight family bonds and loyalty might (also) have played a role?

Another wonderful example of solidarity comes from Elizabeth Laidler's study area in Guyana, as related in her book *The River Wolf*. A group of local hunters, while pursuing tapir, disturbed a family of six otters, including two cubs barely able to swim. By firing their guns in the air, the men succeeded in scaring off the four older animals and captured the cubs, intending to rear them as pets. The otter group gave chase but the hunters' boat, equipped with an outboard engine, easily outdistanced them. The men made camp seven or eight miles further and kept the cubs under a basket weighed down by large stones. About two in the morning, the men were roused by a tremendous noise: the family had returned to rescue the cubs. All six animals were spotted in the beam of a torch, making their escape.

DENS

Giant otters are almost exclusively diurnal, that is, active only during the day, between dawn and dusk. Nights are usually spent together inside a den excavated in the river or lake bank, frequently under root systems or fallen trees with vegetation cover overhead. The den consists of one or more linked chambers several square metres in size. There may be a backdoor tunnel as well as a main entrance, and small air vents may be present. Once we discovered a den with a submerged entrance; we could hear the gurgling of water as the otters passed through, followed seconds later by the appearance of their heads above the surface.

An active giant otter den is easily recognised by a muddy slide or path that leads from the entrance to the water's edge, and by the presence of a nearby communal latrine. Fresh tracks, lack of leaf litter, trampled vegetation, the presence of insects, and a strong, fishy smell all indicate that a den or latrine is in use. A den may be used for one night only or for several nights in a row, and some dens are used once and then abandoned while others may be used for decades by several generations of otters.

Dens presumably afford protection against bad weather and predators, and are also used for birthing and raising young cubs. In some parts of the giant otter's range, however, such as in the Balbina reservoir in Brazil, in swamps around Russell Lake in Guyana, and in reed marshes in Suriname, giant otter families sleep above ground in stands of dense vegetation, using beds formed by their own bodies. In these areas dens are only used for cub rearing. Thus, habitat type, physical characteristics of banks such as slope, stability, and vegetation cover, and vulnerability to flooding and erosion probably influence the presence of dens.

The reproductive male marks the latrine after all other members of the group have used it, by carefully spreading scat and urine with circular, shuffling movements of his webbed feet. (FH)

VOCALISATIONS

Giant otters have a sophisticated communication system that reflects the species' complex social organisation. More than twenty distinct types of vocalisations have been described, used in four major contexts: for contact and coordination, to threaten or express alarm, for begging, and during mating and nursing. Anything unexpected or strange will be met with an alarmed or warning series of explosive exhalations — *Hah!* — and snorts — *Brr, brr!* — while the otter or family periscopes to obtain a better view. Subtle gradations in these sounds probably signal different types of danger, such as caimans, humans, or a strange otter, as well as different levels of urgency. Much like human voices, otter vocalisations and especially snorts, one of the most frequent of giant otter sounds, probably also convey information about the identity, size, age, and sex of the individuals uttering them. Furthermore, two studies in zoos have shown that giant otters make at least one vocalisation underwater, a very low frequency sound that is assumed to act as a cohesion call.

A mother will reassure her young with a constant, low *hrrum*, almost a purr, or initiate a new activity or change in direction with a lilting version of the same sound. Cubs beg for fish from their older siblings with ear-splitting shrieks that can be heard a hundred metres away. The reluctant sibling may growl fiercely in response. When a cub eventually receives or steals a morsel of fish, it will garble loudly in excitement, waving its tail and kicking its hind feet to keep others at bay. And when one otter wails in high alarm, for example, when it bumps into a black caiman, or calls out after becoming separated from the rest of the group, all family members rush together and utter wavering screams.

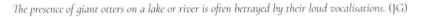

The presence of giant otters on a lake or river is often betrayed by their loud vocalisations. (JG)

SCENT-MARKING

Sound communication is important mainly within the confines of the family territory because, in contrast to wolves (whose howls travel at least 10 kilometres), lions (with roars heard from eight kilometres away), and howler monkeys (4.8 kilometres), the caterwauling of giant otters probably carries over no more than several hundred metres. However, the silent language of smells is equally if not more powerful, as well as longer-lasting, than vocal exchanges.

On the shorelines of rivers and lakes within their home range, giant otters create *campsites*. These are irregularly-shaped patches of land several square metres in size that have been swept clear of leaf litter and vegetation by the otters, and which are used for scent-marking, drying out, resting, and grooming. They are usually positioned well above water level where flooding is less likely, and directly next to the water body, often in a prominent, highly visible site such as a confluence of a stream, on a beach, or at a sharp river bend. They are also frequently associated with cross-over points – locations where giant otters habitually take short cuts over land – between two water bodies or across a river meander.

All campsites have one or more communal marking areas of varying freshness, known as middens or latrines and usually characterised by a layer of fish scales and other hard fish parts excreted by the otters. This is why campsites are often confused by local people with places where otters eat their prey. When recently used, the latrine's odour is powerful and fishy and may carry far. Large numbers of insects – sweat and honey bees, ants, butterflies, and flies – arrive within minutes of the otters leaving. The soil is damp or muddy, and nearby twigs and saplings look bedraggled, stripped, chewed, or muddy. Latrines are to giant otters what lamp posts are to dogs.

Otters scent-mark several times a day – in the mornings before going hunting, at least once during hunting sessions, and in the late afternoons, before entering the den for the night – and may visit several different campsites during a day. Visits tend to be brief, under 10 minutes in duration, with all members of the group sniffing, defecating, and urinating on the latrine, followed by thorough trampling of the faeces or *scat*. Giant otter scats are loose, dark-greenish deposits, consisting mostly of scales and other fish hard parts such as vertebrae, otoliths, teeth, and large spines, as well as thick mucus. The latter covers the otter's alimentary canal and intestine and helps protect it against abrasions and punctures. Glands on either side of the anus produce a strong-smelling secretion, either during defecation or when the otter is suddenly startled.

Almost all dens will have a campsite or, at the least, a latrine nearby, whereas many campsites are not associated with a den. Like dens, a campsite may be used once only and then never again, or for many years, even decades, by different generations or groups. For giant otter researchers, dens and campsites are a reliable and easy way to determine whether a water body has been or is being occupied by a giant otter group. Sometimes all we have to do is follow our noses.

Campsites are created on high ground, with plenty of overhanging vegetation to provide shade and cover, and at strategic locations in a family's home range. (Top, FH; bottom, JG)

HOME RANGES AND TERRITORIES

A giant otter home range is the area routinely inhabited and used by a group for food gathering, mating, and caring for its young. The *home range* includes a core area where the family spends the bulk of its time, zones outside the core area that are visited occasionally, and transit routes between these areas. It does not necessarily imply exclusive use. The *core area* of the home range, however, also referred to as the territory, is one of exclusive use from which other groups stay away or are excluded. This implies priority access to resources that are critical to ensure successful reproduction – the key function of territoriality. Territories are maintained through defence and scent-marking activities. In seasonally flooded areas, only the exclusive territories are defended throughout the dry season, whereas they are apparently abandoned during the rainy season when giant otters follow fish into the flooded forests.

DIET AND HUNTING

Giant otters eat almost exclusively fish. Though occasionally reported by others, I have never personally observed them taking aquatic birds, amphibians, or small mammals. Once we found crab remains on a latrine but crustaceans clearly do not play an important role in giant otter diet. We have witnessed the capture of a yellow

Giant otters eat mostly fish... (JMR)

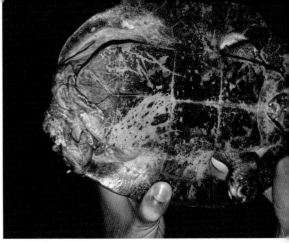

Above left: *... but are not averse to trying out the occasional turtle...* (RS)

Above right: *... though the experience can be frustrating since they are unable to break open the turtle's shell.* (FH)

Left: *Black caimans (Melanosuchus niger) and giant otters have an uneasy relationship, with one occasionally falling victim to the other. This is a juvenile.* (JG)

Below: *A young black caiman is unlucky this time.* (FH)

spotted side-necked turtle (*Podocnemis unifilis*) on three occasions; only the legs and head were chewed, with a combination of curiosity and frustration. Other researchers have reported giants opportunistically eating snakes and even molluscs, and one study in the Pantanal documented them feeding regularly on sub adult yacare caimans (*Caiman yacare*). This is unusual, however, and may have been due to severe drought conditions and resource scarcity in the area. Once, in Manu, we saw a giant otter snatch and eat a juvenile black caiman (*Melanosuchus niger*), and on a separate occasion attempt to capture one:

'The otters start to fish in front of the den. One individual that has swum roughly thirty metres further along the shore catches a young caiman, approximately forty centimetres in length. The giant otter returns towards the den, already eating its prey as it utters distress sounds. A large black caiman appears, presumably the mother, and charges towards the otters. The group reacts and several members begin the high alarm call. The caiman splashes in threat and then disappears. The giant otter devours the small caiman completely, while a sub adult otter begs nearby.'

Field notes, Cocha Salvador, 16 August 2005

'On the way back to the den, one giant otter separates from the group, climbs onto the lake bank, and begins to search in the shoreline vegetation. A small black caiman rushes into the water and swims rapidly towards overhanging leafy branches. The giant otter pursues it, and caiman distress sounds come from behind the foliage. At this point, a large black caiman appears and charges towards the overhanging vegetation. The giant otter emerges, in fast evasive action, without the young caiman.'

Field notes, Cocha Salvador, 25 August 2005

Giant otters characteristically hunt as a group, with individuals rarely becoming separated for long; the rest of the family maintains a distance which permits visual or at least acoustic contact. Prey is always consumed by its captor alone, except during cub-rearing when fish caught by sub adults or adults are offered to the cubs, or when young otters snatch fish from other members of the group. The fish is grasped between the forepaws and eaten head first to incapacitate it, the otter chewing rapidly and audibly, from side to side. The only parts that are sometimes discarded are the gill arches and the intestines. Small fish are eaten while swimming in the water near the point of capture, while larger prey are seized near the head and transported to the shore. Only large fish are ever eaten by several otters simultaneously. Giant otters spend between five and a half to seven hours (approximately 60%) of their day hunting, and each otter consumes between three and four kilograms of fish per day. This represents between 10% and 15% of the river wolf's body weight.

Giant otters employ different forms of fishing depending on water depth and microhabitat type. They search under submerged tree logs; forage under floating vegetation, amongst aquatic grasses, and in seasonally flooded forest; and hunt in open water bodies. These foraging methods differ in the cohesiveness of group members, the form of the dive, the level of excitement and vocalisation, and the prey catch success rate per otter. In clear water, and especially in the shallows, giant otters may float or move slowly with eyes open, scanning the surroundings for fish, before launching into high speed and noisy chases, twisting and lunging just under the surface. Deep water fishing involves steeper and more synchronised dives. In deep water or water with poor visibility, giants may depend on the tactile sense of their facial whiskers, scattering a school of fish and selecting their victim at the very last moment, typically going for the closest prey and pursuing it vigorously. Or they may approach from behind and below, taking advantage of a blind spot for most fish. This sometimes results in an explosive spray of fish above water, as they desperately seek to avoid capture.

PREDATORS

Giant otters appear to have few predators. They are themselves one of the region's largest carnivores and are group-living, making them a force to be reckoned with. When a family encounters a potential threat, all members, except the very young,

Black caimans can grow to a length of six metres, more than three times that of a giant otter. (JG)

The spectacled or white caiman is probably a less important predator. (RS)

A jaguar, on the other hand, is quite capable of launching itself into the water in pursuit of a giant otter. (JMR)

investigate and try to intimidate the intruder into retreating. This mobbing behaviour ranges from merely calling attention to the presence of the danger, to all-out harassment, chasing, and attacking. A black caiman (*Melanosuchus niger*), white caiman (*Caiman crocodilus*), anaconda (*Eunectes murinus*), or jaguar (*Panthera onca*) risks severe injury or death by targeting a group of giant otters. Nonetheless, online video footage showing a jaguar launching itself from a bank into the Cuiaba River, Brazil, in a (failed) attempt to catch one of the younger

Giant otters take every opportunity to put caimans in their place. Here an otter nips the tail of a caiman... (ND)

... and jumps away when it swings round to face its attacker. (ND)

members of an otter family, clearly demonstrates that big cats are sometimes prepared to take a risk. In the Balbina hydroelectric reservoir, Brazil, that risk paid off: a solitary radio tagged otter was found dead in a shelter among dense vegetation with jaguar tracks around her carcass. Several other online video interactions between a jaguar and a giant otter group, however, end with the cat either reluctantly moving away in the face of persistent mobbing, or launching itself into the water and coming up empty-pawed.

Black caimans, which can reach a length more than three times that of a giant otter, may also pose a serious threat. The species sometimes occurs in high densities. On most oxbow lakes in Manu, for example, between one and five black caimans are counted for every 100 metres of shoreline. Typically, as the otters hunt along the shore, they are so engrossed that they find themselves almost on top of the caiman before they discover it. Usually, when harassed repeatedly by the otters, the caiman either quietly submerges and swims to deeper water or bluff splashes in warning before partially retreating to the shore in an attempt to protect its belly and flanks. However, occasionally encounters are more serious:

'... At 9:50 am, while fishing under overhanging vegetation, several otters started the loud wavering call associated with group alarm. This was followed by violent splashing and repeated charges by the otters towards a focal point deep in the shadows. Several otters went on shore and then re-entered the fray. After nearly five minutes of intense activity, a caiman about twice the length of the giant otters erupted from the water, scrambled over a semi-submerged log, and swam away from the scene. All ten members of the otter family left the water and crossed over land to another part of the lake close to their main den, where they resumed hunting. At 10:25 am one otter separated from the group and returned to the den. It lingered in the water for a couple of minutes before limping onto the shore. At this point we saw the otter had sustained serious injuries to its right front leg. When on land, the otter avoided putting weight on it, and held it up close to its chest. The otter entered the den and was not seen again until the next morning.'

Field notes, Cocha Cashu, 13 October 2004.

In the days following the attack, the injured otter, which eventually fully recovered, was charged by black caimans on three further occasions.

Other black caiman-otter encounters may end very differently. In dramatic footage filmed on Cocha Salvador, Manu National Park, for BBC2's *Natural World* series, a family of six adult giant otters with three cubs tries to intimidate a large black caiman into moving away from its den but the caiman makes the grave mistake of putting

The anaconda (Eunectes murinus) is a potential predator of a young or inattentive giant otter. (FH)

up a fight. The otters manage to overpower the caiman and eventually kill it, after a battle lasting one hour. Yet, while it is clearly conceivable that caimans are capable of preying on giant otters, especially cubs or solitary dispersers, they may actually be more important as indirect competitors for food since they, too, eat mostly fish.

Anacondas are probably more dangerous as predators of young giant otters, especially if the latter have become separated from the rest of the group. There have been several reports of pet Neotropical otters being taken by anacondas. Laidler witnessed an aggressive encounter between a large anaconda and a family of six giant otters in her study area in Guyana:

'The anaconda, about 12 centimetres in diameter and 5 metres long, was looped around the branches of a half-drowned tree near the edge of the bank. The giant otter family had formed a rough semi-circle around the snake and the four adult members – presumably the parents and their sub adult offspring – made repeated sallies towards it, caterwauling continuously. The two smaller juveniles tended to keep behind the cordon of adults. The anaconda disappeared into the underbrush on the bank after about five minutes of the mobbing behaviour.'

From Elizabeth Laidler's 1984 doctorate dissertation

Otters never seem to look upwards in search of danger. This would suggest that large raptors like the harpy eagle or crested eagle do not pose a threat. Observations at Cocha Cashu, in Manu National Park, of giant otters in the presence of a drone flying overhead, seemed to confirm this. There was no visible reaction to the drone at heights of 15 metres or more, despite its noise, and even at 10 metres the reaction was minimal,

Raptors, like this great black-hawk (Buteogallus urubitinga) do not seem to present a danger to giant otters. (JG)

with one otter that was eating a fish looking up and backing away slightly, then turning on its back to watch the drone while continuing to eat its fish. No individuals periscoped or otherwise expressed alarm. It appears, then, that giant otters do not have reason to fear aerial predators.

POPULATION STRUCTURE AND GROUP SIZE

Most mustelids live solitarily and few live in groups. The giant otter, however, is a highly social species generally living in close-knit families each consisting of a monogamous breeding pair plus their offspring of various years. In addition to family groups with defended territories (known as *resident* groups), a typical giant otter population also includes dispersers, referred to as *transients*, who have left their natal (birth) groups, normally after reaching sexual maturity, or who have lost a mate. Although often solitary, dispersers may form temporary, non-breeding associations – transient groups – that do not have an established territory. During our research in Manu, lone and group transients made up an average of 13% of the population: the bulk of the population therefore consists of family groups.

Groups number between two and a maximum of 16 individuals, with an average group size of five or six. Resident group size varies with habitat type and is naturally limited by the balance between births of cubs and dispersal of young adults. Reports

The maximum number of otters I've seen out on a fallen tree is 10. This family of eight on Cocha Cashu, in Manu National Park, comes close. (FH)

of so-called 'supergroups' of up to 20 animals are very rare, and may have been a consequence of a group being forced into the neighbouring territory of a second group, while fleeing from the approach of a threat such as a noisy boat. It is also not unusual for local people to overestimate the number of otters in a group during a short sighting, probably due to the otters' habit of repeatedly submerging and surfacing elsewhere.

HABITAT PREFERENCES

The giant otter is found in a wide variety of lowland habitats: in extensive wetlands such as the Brazilian Pantanal; in huge man-made lakes like the Balbina reservoir, also in Brazil; or in blackwater creeks and flooded forest in the Guianas. Blackwaters are characteristic of still or slow-flowing freshwater systems, especially those based on clay soil, and have strikingly low levels of suspended sediment loads. Their translucent, dark brown colour, like that of tea, is due to the leaching of substances from leaf litter, vegetation, and humus in the forest soil. Blackwater creeks also lack suspended plankton and aquatic insects, yet fish are nonetheless abundant due to debris supplied by the overhanging forest — fruits, insects, leaves, and branches — which provides them with food and shelter.

In south-eastern Peru whitewater bodies dominate, so-called due to the sediments which remain in constant suspension and as a result of which transparency is low and visibility poor, from a few centimetres in the rainy season to about half a metre in the

Giants live in a variety of habitats, from tranquil open oxbow lakes... (JG)

... to ones that are becoming overgrown with aquatic vegetation... (JG)

... to small whitewater rivers and meandering streams... (FH)

... or large blackwater rivers... (JMR)

... and *Mauritia flexuosa* palm swamps. Giant otter conservation implies the conservation of a great diversity of wetland habitats. (FH)

dry season. Rather than rivers, otters prefer the associated small lakes or *cochas*, former river meanders that are cut off through erosion and that can persist as distinct bodies of water for decades or centuries, but which remain connected to the parent river to varying degrees, with some experiencing exchange of river nutrients and fish only during the highest floods. With an abundance of overhanging vegetation providing organic input, these tranquil lakes are nutrient rich and highly productive; they may have four times as much fish biomass per unit area than their associated river channels.

Oxbow lakes have other clear advantages over river environments: water current is negligible, transparency is greater (average visibility is 67 centimetres, with a maximum of 135 centimetres), and changes in water level are less extreme. Thus, rivers are often solely used by otters as a means to travel from one lake to another. However, in isolated regions where there is little human presence and where oxbow lakes are infrequent, the rivers and their tributaries may themselves be inhabited by giant otters on a permanent basis. This is also the case, for example, on the Orinoco River on the Colombian-Venezuelan border and on the Meta River where giant otters are present in whitewaters with a high sediment load, with dens and campsites located in rocky zones rather than on earthen banks.

In all studies, key factors influencing giant otter habitat preference were found to be low human disturbance, the presence of non-floodable banks with good vegetation cover for establishing dens and latrines, and, most importantly, easy access year round to fishing sites with an abundance of vulnerable prey in relatively shallow waters. Many parts of the giant otter's distribution range, though not all, experience heavy rainfall and widespread lateral flooding during the wet season. These drastic fluctuations in water level have profound effects on the feeding, reproduction, and dispersal of fish. During high water phases, when more food is available, fish migrate to spawning grounds in the flooded forest and their predators, such as the giant otter, are forced to follow. Seasonality factors thus affect the distribution and biomass of fish populations.

DISTRIBUTION RANGE

Giant otters are endemic to South America and were once widely distributed throughout the lowlands east of the Andes mountains in the Orinoco, Amazonas, and Parana basins, and in the three Guianas. Currently, the giant otter's range is much reduced, having contracted by more than a third over the last century, with populations completely eliminated in many localised areas within the remainder of its distribution. The species is considered extinct in Uruguay and Argentina, and is reduced to a single, tiny population in Paraguay, occupying less than 2% of its former distribution range. Important subpopulations are found in the Pantanal and parts of the Brazilian Amazon and in the Guianas – Suriname, Guyana, and French Guiana – although the future of the species in these countries is not as secure as it once was due to the expansion of gold mining activities. In French Guiana,

Actual and historical distribution range of the giant otter

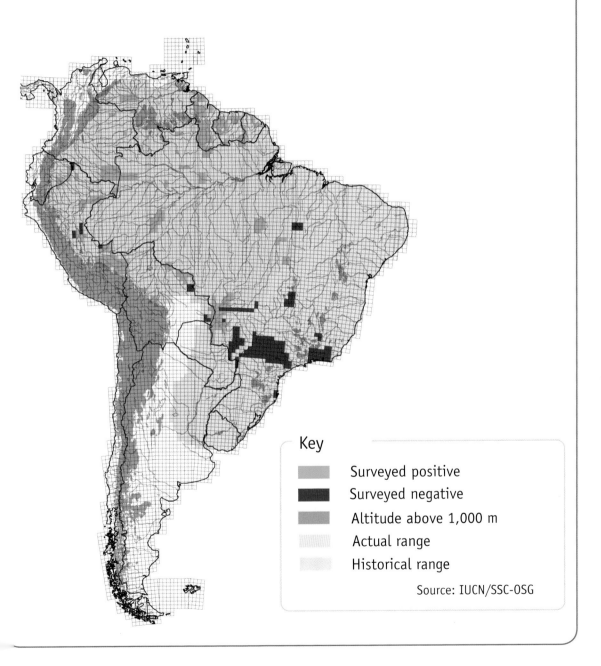

Key

- Surveyed positive
- Surveyed negative
- Altitude above 1,000 m
- Actual range
- Historical range

Source: IUCN/SSC-OSG

for example, 212 hectares of forest were impacted by miners in 1990, compared to more than 4,000 hectares in 2000, 11,500 hectares in 2006, and 21,500 hectares in 2010. The otter population of Venezuela is one of the least studied.

The current total wild population is unknown and we do not know if it is increasing or not. Evidence indicates that some sub populations are recovering, especially in remote, undisturbed, or protected areas in northern Peru, the north-eastern Ecuadorian Amazon, and the Pantanal. In other regions, such as in the Department of Madre de Dios in south-eastern Peru and in western Colombia, populations are thought to be on the decline. The 2015 IUCN Red List assessment for the giant otter states that population estimates based on surveys exist for only a few areas: in the Brazilian Pantanal up to 5,000 individuals; in Madre de Dios, 180 to 400 animals (the majority in protected areas); in the Cantao State Park, Brazil, 31 individuals; in Amana, Brazil, 75 individuals; in the Balbina reservoir, Brazil, at least 130 animals; in Araguaia, Brazil, 54 individuals; and in Yasuní National Park, Ecuador, 32 animals. Most of these sub populations remain isolated from each other.

Country population estimates have been made for Bolivia: in the north-west (Madre de Dios-Beni sub-basin), 60 individuals in 185,805 square kilometres; in the Pantanal (Paraguay sub-basin), 50 individuals in 118,031 square kilometres; and in the north-east (Itenez sub-basin), 600 individuals in 186,460 square kilometres, totalling an estimated 700 animals. In Ecuador there are considered to be fewer than 250; in French Guiana at least 200; and in Paraguay only a maximum of 32 (though the population is thought to be increasing).

GIANT OTTERS: THE BIG EXCEPTION

Most animals of the tropical rainforest in South America are small, seldom seen, solitary, and nocturnal. The giant otter — the largest and among the heaviest of the world's 13 otter species — is one exception. They are longer in body length than many humans, live in highly social groups, and are exclusively diurnal. While other terrestrial apex predators like the jaguar or puma must cover enormous areas of several thousand hectares to find sufficient prey, giant otters manage to thrive in small lakes where there is 150 times less space per individual compared to the terrestrial hunters. Yet their overall density is low, roughly 100 individuals in the 1.7 million hectare Manu National Park, a protected area which is likely to harbour at least 400 jaguars. Why?

The giant otter is the outcome of a perfect niche adaptation. In an environment where most nutrients are fixed in living systems (plants and insects), where the soil is poor and the struggle for life has resulted in extraordinary biodiversity, and where predator pressure is high and there is little to eat for most mammals, many species are forced to be solitary creatures of the night that were unable to grow large in evolutionary time. However, nutrients are leached by heavy rains and powerful rivers and are sometimes collected in wetlands, especially in cut-off meanders that are the oxbow lakes. Together with an impressive input of organic material from the forest (leaves, fruits, insects), this leads to an exceptional diversity and abundance of fish species. Otters are aquatic predators that opted for a 'land' of milk and honey. The high prey density enables them to live in groups, to enjoy greater hunting success, to share care for their young, and to fend off all other predators.

However, the 'green desert' – the rainforest – covers a vast area, while the land of milk and honey is small in comparison. This is why the density of giant otters is so low.

Unfortunately, water is not the easiest medium for any mammal to live in. It is dense, movement costs a lot of energy, little oxygen is available, and heat loss is 25 times greater than in air (otters do not have an insulating fat layer). Scientific studies on the Eurasian otter (*Lutra lutra*) have shown that this species lives on the edge. In cold water, it only just manages to catch enough prey to survive. If prey density goes down, loss of energy while searching for prey is greater than that gained by eating, especially since otters are not behavioural energy savers. Possibly, the Eurasian otter, too, would have 'preferred' to be

The green desert (from a giant otter's perspective). (WW)

large, particularly since energy loss is reduced when body size is greater, due to the surface to volume ratio. But large animals need a lot of food (three to four kilograms per day for an adult giant otter) and it is impossible to catch so much fish in cold European waters. Their Neotropical relatives, however, have two significant environmental advantages: the water is warm year-round (28.5 degrees Celsius on average in Manu National Park) and there is plenty of fish. This enabled the giant otter to grow to a size that makes jaguars and caimans think twice about attacking them. Yes, fights still occur but these are dangerous for both predator and prey. The otters did not need to hunt at night and could fish by sight in daylight, using energy-intensive hunting methods with a high success rate, in habitats with an abundance of prey, enabling group living with all its added advantages.

However, what made them once so successful – their ability to thrive in rivers and lakes, the richest feeding grounds for a predator in the Neotropics – today makes giant otters so vulnerable to anthropogenic impacts. Rivers are the roads of the Amazon, where human encroachment invariably begins and expands like bacteria in a petri dish, where deforestation, gold mining, and overfishing pressure is most intense. The future for the giant otter is cloudy. Losing the giant otter would mean losing one of the highlights of evolution.

Dr. Christof Schenck
Director, Frankfurt Zoological Society

Communication

The torrential rain that delayed our departure from camp at last dwindles to a fine mist. Half an hour later, a watery sun glints on polished leaves and highlights drops trembling at their tips. The forest is hushed; the cicadas and crickets seem chastened by the downpour. We set forth in subdued anticipation. People rarely visit Peru's Manu National Park during the wet season and the neglected trail beneath our feet is a level, cleansed canvas. Any animal tracks that we encounter will be fresh.

Soon, Frank points silently at the ground by his boots. Expecting the fairly commonplace signature of a peccary or agouti, I glance over his shoulder and am confronted with a perfect jaguar track. All toe pads are clearly outlined, the edges crisp. It is as though the cat deliberately and carefully placed his paw in the saturated rainforest soil. Here I am, he says. The immediacy of the jaguar's presence is palpable

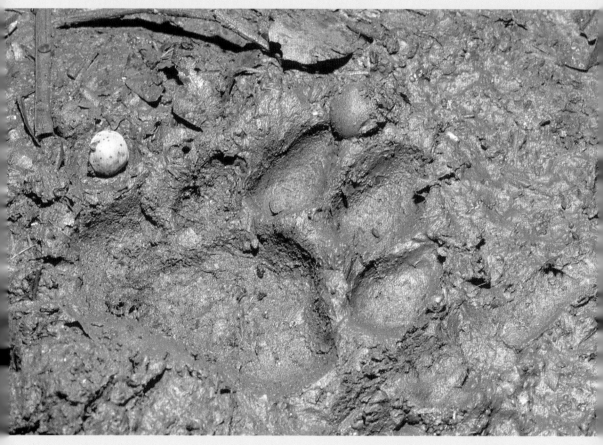

'All toe pads are clearly outlined, the edges crisp.' (FH)

This photo was taken a week after the events of this story, and is of the same half-tailed jaguar on the same platform. (FH)

and I scan the vegetation, convinced I will glimpse a crouching form. Frank holds a finger against his lips. If we're quiet we might be lucky, his eyes tell me. I nod in agreement.

A short while later, another set of imprints, like exclamation marks. My heart beats faster. Our heightened senses grope for a whisper of sound, a twitching leaf. In my mind's eye, I watch the jaguar amble over tangled tree roots, black rosettes sliding over powerful shoulders. See, here he has stopped to scrape restlessly at the earth. Perhaps to listen to the distant duets of dusky titi monkeys, just as we are now. Frank glances at me and I know the tension in his face is mirrored in my own. We tread quietly, the damp leaf litter for once not betraying us.

But the tracks vanish as suddenly as they appeared. I scrutinize the forest floor, expecting to find another sign. Nothing. An increasing feeling of disappointment, almost of loss, replaces my excitement. Frank shrugs in resignation when I look at him. Elusive as ever, the jaguar has stepped out of our narrow world and has entered the jungle where we cannot follow.

The afternoon loses some of its magic as we continue along the path. We clamber over fallen tree trunks, skirt around a frantic horde of fiery red ants. Has their nest been flooded? A wood quail explodes from the nearby shrubs as we pass. I reflect wryly, if that had happened moments earlier, my heart would have stopped. My thoughts wander to the giant otter family we are hoping to find on Lake Otorongo. So do Frank's, I notice, because he speeds up a little and sweat begins to prickle my forehead. I am grateful for the cool forest air; on the water the heat will be stunning despite the sun's late arrival.

As we approach the shore, without warning, Frank stops dead. An involuntary grunt escapes him. I am trying to avoid trampling the ant trail, and almost stumble into him. His hand reaches for mine, urging me to be still. Taken aback, I look up. Straight into the taut, yellow eyes of a jaguar.

We are all transfixed. I cannot comprehend that he is actually there, barely five metres away. He growls softly. At the sound, joy thrills through my every nerve. I begin to take in details, how the jaguar is half lying down, his upper body turned towards us. I realize that, eager to escape the soaked jungle, he sought out the lake observation pier and was basking in the sun's warmth until jolted awake by our abrupt arrival.

Seconds elapse. We stand immobile, pinned by his unwavering stare. Finally, he blinks, breaking the spell. Inch by inch, the jaguar lifts a paw, indicating his wish to leave. I sense he feels trapped because we are unintentionally blocking his only exit. Slowly grasping Frank by his shirt, I motion him to step backwards a few paces. There we await the jaguar's next move.

Reassured, he walks towards the entrance of the platform. I smile when, remembering to affect unconcern, he pauses to rub his broad head against a wooden cross-beam, like a friendly housecat. Then he glides leisurely down onto the trail, which we now share. The jaguar is full grown, in splendid shape, half-tailed. Without looking back, he soundlessly merges into the greenery. All too soon, he is gone.

My breath whooshes out and I turn to Frank in jubilation. He grins at me. Hours later, I am still aglow with our experience. No previous big cat sighting in the rainforest has conveyed such a heady awareness of having, somehow ... *communicated*.

CHAPTER TWO

A Day with the Family

DAWN BREAKS ON COCHA OTORONGO

*I*t is 5:15 am and the otters are stirring in their den. A series of soft cooing sounds, followed by the characteristic 'Let's go' hum, indicates the family is ready to start the day. A moment later, out comes Isla, the breeding female. She sniffs the latrine area in front of the den thoroughly and is soon joined by Hueco, her partner. Together they urinate and defecate on the latrine, their broad, flattened tails held high, before thoroughly trampling and mixing their scat with those that have accumulated overnight. The semicircular, sweeping movements of their forepaws and the simultaneous shuffling of their hind legs combine to resemble a comical scent-marking dance.

A third otter appears at the entrance of the den. It is Harpon, named after the arrow head outlined on his throat. Unlike his parents, he pauses only briefly to defecate, not lingering to mix

The otter family emerges from the den at dawn and spends the next ten minutes or so on the latrine in front of the entrance before embarking on the day's activities. (FH)

Early morning on an oxbow lake. These fish-rich havens provide high quality habitat for giant otters. (ABT)

his scat, and is followed in rapid succession by four other otters, all of whom eagerly rush into the water after a quick, obligatory stop on the latrine. Hueco does the work for them, waddling once more over the latrine while simultaneously dribbling urine. Isla enters the water sedately and begins to groom herself on a submerged log while she waits for Hueco; he is the last to leave the den site. Isla hums once and the group sets off along the shoreline, just as a gossamer mist begins to lift from the surface of the lake.

SLEEPING SITES

A group may alternate between several dens in its home range. It is not clear why giant otters regularly change dens. A likely reason could be to take advantage of particularly rich prey patches. Otters might also move to another den if these become infested with parasites or biting insects, or when a cub dies inside. In captivity, excessive moisture in the nest box (from their fur after leaving the water) was identified as an important reason during the rearing of cubs, perhaps to protect them from bacterial infections. Stress caused by human disturbance frequently motivates a change of den in captivity and has also been reported in the field: giant otter researchers may themselves unwittingly prompt a den change. In the wild, an additional trigger could be the nearby presence of predators: large black caiman are sometimes observed to hang around an otter den, whether intentionally

When re-using an old den, it is first energetically cleaned out. Hueco catches the brunt of Isla's cleaning efforts. (FH)

A change of dens when cubs are small is risky and the mother is quick to install them into their new home. (JMR)

or accidentally. Den switching with newborn cubs is particularly risky and groups go about this in a business-like manner:

'9:00 am. We find the group just as it is in the process of taking two cubs from the first den to a new den approximately four hundred metres further along the shore. Most, if not all otters accompany the two carrying, in a tight formation. On depositing the two cubs, five otters immediately head back to the first den, returning with three more babies in their mouths. The otters travel side by side and in haste, not allowing themselves to be distracted. Swimming phases are alternated with a series of shallow dives during which the cubs are carried underwater. On re-surfacing, we can hear the querulous squeaks of the cubs. Then all enter the new den.'

Field notes, Cocha Salvador, 31 October 2002

AS THE FOREST AWAKENS

The seven otters begin to hunt along the shoreline, nosing under submerged forest debris where leafy branches of trees and shrubs grow down to the waterline, or diving in the shallows. They advance slowly and methodically, amidst much noise and splashing. After a brief chase, Hueco captures a large fish and seeks out a submerged tree log on which to rest while he eats. He grasps his catch with his webbed feet, and, beginning with the head, tears off chunks of flesh with powerful and rapid biting movements. He eats with concentration and relish. The rest of the group does not wait for him; each otter is intent on filling its own belly. Hueco finishes his fish, checks that he is not leaving a tasty morsel behind and quickly catches up with his family. Suddenly, there is a small commotion by the shoreline. Isla and Harpon are snorting at something. A caiman? But they soon resume hunting: it was only a curious capuchin monkey. Three cormorants swim at the fringes of the group, snapping up any fleeing catfish, and a snowy egret paces expectantly along the shore.

After an hour or so, Isla leads the family to deeper water mid-lake. Here they dive randomly for longer moments and are more spaced out. Harpon's brother captures a boca chico which is small

Giant otters eat almost exclusively fish. Starting with the head is the best way to prevent a slippery prize from escaping or biting back. (FH)

Piranhas are also on the giant otter menu. (ABT)

Giants share their home with a multitude of creatures. Monkeys, like this capuchin, like to feed on fruits in shoreline vegetation. (JG)

enough to devour above water while swimming on his back. In seconds the fish is gone. Then the otters hunt in earnest. The group assembles in a small area and they begin a series of rapid, leaping dives, their bodies leaving the water almost entirely on surfacing after each dive. They have found a school of fish and their aim is to confuse and tire their prey. The technique works: four otters emerge almost simultaneously with fish in their mouths and all head towards the shore. The remaining members of the group continue to porpoise close together, trying to secure catches of their own.

FISH PREFERENCES

Giant otters feed almost exclusively on fish, generally between 7 and 30 centimetres in length, but sometimes up to a metre long. Preferred species are from the orders Characiformes, Perciformes, and Siluriformes. In open water, such as the central or deepest parts of lakes, giant otters may catch detritivores from the Characidae, Curimatidae, and Prochilontidae families that tend to form multi-species schools. Another much favoured family is the Cichlidae which are caught in the shallows. These fish, measuring up to 20 centimetres, are territorial and insectivorous, lying immobile on the bottom and having a tendency to flee only at the last moment. The Anostomidae are also small to medium-sized, typically bottom-feeding detritivores, while *Hoplias malabaricus* is a bottom-dwelling ambush predator. Its habit of sitting and waiting makes it a frequent giant otter prey item. The nocturnal Gymnotids shelter in the mud and roots of plants among floating islands and in cavities of logs. Then there are the catfish of the Pimelodidae, Loricariidae, and Doradidae families. The former grow to a large size and on one occasion we observed an entire otter family feeding together on a single fish. The Loricariidae are slow-moving, heavily armoured catfish with a sucker mouth. Although not a preferred prey item, they are easily caught and make suitable practice prey for otter cubs learning to hunt.

In general, fish species that favour slow flowing or still water shoreline microhabitats with floating vegetation and woody debris, and that have sedentary, territorial, or ambush hunting habits — such as the cichlids, *Hoplias malabaricus*, and gymnotids — tend to dominate giant otter diet, as does the schooling *Prochilodus*. Individual otters and otter families may show distinct preferences for certain fish species, however, with one group perhaps displaying a greater reliance on cichlid prey, and another family tending to prefer piranha (*Serrasalmus* species).

Scat analysis, involving the identification of fish scales and other hard parts in giant otter faeces, have confirmed that giants specialize in fish throughout their distribution range. After identifying 71,000 scales, a study found that giant otters in oxbow lakes in south-eastern Peru consume at least 21 different fish species but that they hunt prey selectively. Only eight species formed 97% of their diet. Taxonomic and fish netting experiments have shown that there are more than 200 species of fish as well as extremely high fish densities in these lakes. It seems likely that this high prey density permits giant otters inhabiting oxbow lakes to be specialist hunters, presumably selecting those species that are easiest to catch and offer the highest net calorific return.

Prey sizes between 7 and 30 centimetres are preferred; each otter eats its catch alone, although several members of a group may share a larger fish. (Top left, ND; top right and bottom, JG)

In contrast, a total of 66 fish species were identified in the diet of giant otters living on the Palma Real River, also in south-eastern Peru. The five most important species accounted for 73% of total biomass consumed while eight species made up 85% of the diet. Previous taxonomic work revealed that at least 115 fish species inhabit this river. Although only a handful of species make up a large proportion of the diet, it appears that giant otters generally consume a much broader spectrum of available prey in the Palma Real than they do on oxbow lakes. This may indicate that prey availability in the Palma Real River is lower than in Madre de Dios oxbow lakes, and that giant otters cannot afford to be as selective in the former habitat. Thus, in general, prey species are taken in proportion to their abundance and vulnerability, with otters hunting opportunistically in non-ideal conditions (in marginal habitats, for example, or during the wet season), or more selectively in optimal conditions, during the low water period or in good quality habitat. This pattern was also found to be true elsewhere in the giant otter's range.

HUNTING ZONES

In Manu National Park, two main hunting zones were identified: in shallow, shoreline water with a depth of less than a metre, and in deep, open water at a depth between one and seven metres (the maximum depth of cochas is seven metres while their average depth is two metres). The otters spent 10% more time hunting along the shoreline than in open water, though the fish capture rate was more than three times greater in deep water. It seems, therefore, that shoreline hunting is more energy efficient. About 35% of hunting time in deep water involved a spectacular technique known as *porpoising*, in which otters perform a succession of leaping dives, not unlike dolphins, probably targeting schooling fish. There is more synchrony of movement

The otter family takes a brief respite from the serious business of hunting. (JG)

Hunting mid-lake is less prevalent when cubs are present since they are dependent on the shoreline to eat their prey and to rest. (FH)

Porpoising is a highly effective but energy demanding hunting technique, involving a succession of rapid dives in deep water. (FH)

between family group members during deep water hunting than in shallows hunting, which tends to be a more chaotic form of fishing. Though porpoising appears to be an energetically intensive fishing technique, it resulted in a capture rate more than double that obtained during all other hunting methods combined.

It is worth mentioning that some species seem to take advantage of giant otter hunting activity to capture their own prey. On numerous occasions we have witnessed groups of Neotropic cormorants (*Phalacrocorax brasilianus*) lingering on the fringes of, or even fully participating, in a giant otter fishing bout, snapping up fleeing armoured catfish that are less favoured by giant otters. Various species of herons will also follow an otter family along a shoreline and may wait near an eating otter in hopes of catching small fish seeking scraps. Kingfishers sometimes enter the fray, plunging next to an otter and darting off with a fish. In the early 1980s, in Tuparro National Park, eastern Colombia, primatologist Thomas Defler reported six instances of giant otters and Amazon river dolphins (*Inia geoffrensis*)

Cormorants often accompany the otters during hunting sessions in the hope of catching a fleeing fish. (JG)

A cub begs loudly for the hard-won fish of its older sibling but will be lucky to receive the tail. (JG)

apparently travelling and fishing together, and even suggested they communicated with each other. As far as I'm aware, no study has yet explored these associations between giant otters and other piscivorous species in detail.

GROUP SIZE AND HUNTING SUCCESS

Larger groups spend less time per otter hunting than do smaller groups and have higher fish capture rates. In Cocha Otorongo, for example, a family of eight individuals achieved a catch per unit effort (CPUE) of 5.1; after three members left on reaching sexual maturity, the remaining group of five otters attained a CPUE of 4.2. Dispersers had a lower fish capture rate (2.4 fish per hour) than individuals who hunted in a group (3.8 fish/otter/hour) and therefore compensated by hunting for longer periods.

Though deliberate cooperation was not explicitly observed, it is possible that a degree of accidental or opportunistic cooperation exists between the members of a group and that, as group size increases, so does the efficiency with which prey patches and fish schools are found and exploited. Larger groups may be better able to surround, confuse, and exhaust schools of fish and the probability that fleeing fish are captured by a neighbouring member is greater, surmounting the disadvantage of internal competition for prey.

THE SUN CLIMBS HIGH

It is mid morning and the otters have been hunting without pause for several hours. They are at the end of the lake and Isla is anxious to get back to the den; her teats are turgid with milk. Hueco has other plans. He leaves the water and climbs up the bank to a campsite, a branch snapping under the weight of his body. He goes straight to the latrine, where the leaf litter has been swept aside. Sweat and honey bees buzz drowsily around him as he sniffs at the bare soil, damp and dark with use. Without further ado, he defecates and proceeds to spread the scat, rubbing it into the soil with stiffened forepaws while shuffling his hind legs. Isla climbs up a fallen tree trunk and, using it as an access ramp, walks along its length to where it begins to slope into the water. She then stretches up in a tripod stance and pulls down overhanging foliage and low saplings, feverishly rubbing armfuls between her forepaws and against her chest. At times she almost climbs into the branches, so intent are her efforts to trample and mark the vegetation. Falling back on all fours, she treads the whole lot into the mud. The sound of the flapping of her webbed feet on wet ground fills the air.

Other otters now climb up to the campsite. While one visits the latrine, another explores the edges of the site, rolling in the leaves. Harpon seizes a sapling with his clawed feet and pulls at it, stripping off a leaf in the process. Then he lies on it, and dozes briefly. A butterfly lands on his nose and he twitches in his sleep. Ten minutes later, Isla can no longer contain her impatience and enters the water. She hums insistently. Reluctantly, the other otters join her and the group sets off in the direction of the den.

Several members of the group rummage in leaf litter that has accumulated in an old campsite. It will not be long before every dry leaf has been swept aside and all vegetation has been removed from the latrine area. (FH)

CAMPSITES AND MARKING

Giant otters mark several times a day, vigorously mixing urine, scat, and gland secretions with the substrate, saturating it with scent, and in the process covering themselves and each other with a group odour. Impregnated latrine mud is also rubbed over plants to a height of about one metre; the elevated location of these deposits possibly facilitates wind dispersal of odours.

In choosing the locations of campsites, giant otters select shady, unfloodable banks with little or no cover and low human disturbance. The need for shade is probably due to the low heat tolerance of otters but shade is also helpful if campsites are to stay fresher for longer. Nonetheless, territorial factors probably have a greater influence on campsite distribution than environmental considerations such as shade or cover. Neither the size of individual campsites nor the total number of campsites in a home range appears to be related to group size.

This campsite is in use. Note the mud-bespattered, trampled vegetation and the absence of leaf litter. (FH)

OTHER MARKING BEHAVIOUR

Apart from marking on latrines, four other types of marking behaviour have been observed: (1) scratching at the den entrance without this appearing to have the purpose of enlarging it; (2) trampling on or dragging vegetation between the forepaws and across the chest; (3) rubbing the head, neck, or anal area on a fallen tree in or near the campsite and walking up and down the tree while urinating; and (4) scratching on sections of steep, clayey bank, usually near a den or campsite, producing what is known as *scratch walls*. These deep scratches may be visible for many weeks or months after the den or campsite was last used. Although it is unclear whether giant otters have glands other than anal (for example, interdigital glands), it seems likely that scratch walls serve as a visual rather than a chemical signpost.

WHO MARKS?

All individuals defecate and urinate on latrines but cubs never mix or spread their scat and urine. The breeding pair invariably does so, whereas other adults and the sub adults and juveniles of the group defecate but do not always mix the scat. In Cocha

In Colombia, if sand or soil are absent, stony surfaces will do just fine for scent-marking purposes. (FT)

Otorongo, Manu National Park, just over 80% of all observations of territory marking behaviours were undertaken by the dominant breeding pair. Furthermore, in a study in the southern Pantanal, breeding males marked more frequently than breeding females, with breeding males tending to over-mark the scent deposits of other individuals more than did the alpha females. Over-marks are designed to mask the chemical information left by other individuals, thus reinforcing the over-marker's rights to resources and its dominant and/or reproductive status.

CAMPSITE FUNCTIONS

It seems likely that latrines have an important social function, probably enhancing group bonding and cohesiveness. They may also transmit information regarding the sexual status of group members such as an approaching oestrus or pregnancy, mating receptiveness, dominance hierarchy within a group (or absence of a reproductive animal), territory occupancy even when the resident group is absent, and time elapsed since marking. By using scent-marking to communicate, giant otter groups take pains to avoid meeting one another and largely succeed in doing so. It is tempting to speculate that campsites may serve as a tool, not only of exclusion, but also to show dominance between families, conveying information on group size and composition and hence a group's strength relative to that of its neighbours. Latrines therefore provide a sophisticated means of communication between individuals within a group as well as among groups.

Although the communicative medium of campsites is primarily olfactory, their role in visual communication should not be underestimated. In a habitat such as the Manu floodplain, where lakes rather than rivers are preferred by giant otters, campsites are established mainly on high banks of the cochas. In rivers such as the Palma Real, where lakes are comparatively small and the river itself is the important habitat, campsites are constructed on the river bank, and particularly at the mouths of tributaries, next to big pools, and on access points between the river and small oxbow lakes, all of which tend to be patches of high fish density. Does the prominent location of many campsites provide giant otters with good visibility of the surroundings or are the resident otters using the high visibility of these sites to send a message to foreign otters? Probably both are true.

The distribution of campsites within a home range is not uniform. In some parts of a lakeshore there may be several within fifty metres of each other, while on other long stretches of shore there are none. In the Palma Real we found that campsites were not concentrated at the boundaries of home ranges but were instead distributed at uneven intervals throughout their lengths. Therefore, while there can be little doubt that campsites have a function in delineating territorial boundaries and in excluding other otters from core areas, their distribution is likely to be dictated by additional factors. For instance, it seems possible that otters use campsites to defend and advertise their use of localized resources such as food patches. A recently used campsite acts as a signal that a group has just fished the site. A second group, arriving shortly after, is thus advised to go elsewhere and benefits by not wasting time in a fished site. If the second group does go somewhere else, the first group will also benefit because it can then return to that site before long and find the patch less depleted than if another group had been there in the meantime.

HOME RANGES AND TERRITORIES: STRUCTURE AND SIZE

Information on giant otter home ranges and territories comes from several studies, most conducted during the dry season when conditions are easier for the researcher. In Manu National Park, for example, home ranges typically include one or more oxbow lakes, a nearby stretch of river, and adjacent swamp areas and streams. One or two oxbow lakes form the core area within each home range. Otter groups usually inhabit the same home ranges throughout the year and for several consecutive years. In general, home ranges change little with the seasons, although different microhabitats are used depending on fluctuations in water levels. During the high waters of the rainy season the otters spend more time in Mauritia palm swamps, streams, and flooded forest areas surrounding the lakes, while during the dry season activity is increasingly concentrated on the oxbow lakes themselves. Resident groups tend to have a cyclical pattern of movement, spending most time in the core areas and making partial or full circuits of core areas daily, but paying visits to other parts of their home ranges for several days or weeks at a time. These movements probably reflect the decreasing pay-off in prey catch success of remaining in one part of the home range for too long.

Overlapping of neighbouring home ranges was not observed in Manu, but cannot be discounted as the majority of our observation effort was undertaken in the more accessible core areas of the groups, namely the lakes. Core territory sizes varied between 18.6 hectares (0.2 square kilometres) and 102.9 hectares (one square kilometre). In the latter case, the core territory was also the home range since the resident group was present year-round. We found the density to be approximately five to ten animals per square kilometre of lake.

In the Palma Real watershed, home ranges included a stretch along the main stem of the Palma Real River or its principal tributary the Patuyacu, as well as adjacent small tributaries and tiny oxbow lakes within that stretch. Overlap of home ranges was observed for three of four groups inhabiting the river, although no two otter groups were ever observed using the same stretch of river simultaneously. The length

In south-eastern Peru, oxbow lakes such as this one in Manu National Park are the favoured habitat of giant otters. (JG)

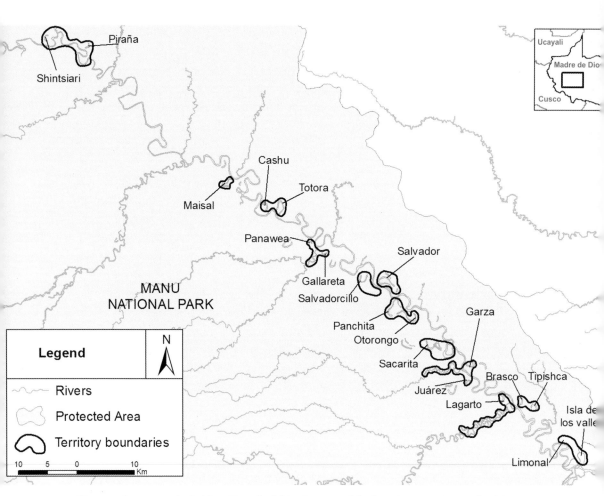

Giant otter home ranges in the Manu River floodplain. One or two lakes form the core territories of each home range.

of dry season home ranges varied from 34 to 79 kilometres, measured along the main channel of the river.

By way of comparison, Nicole Duplaix observed four to five groups in Kaboeri Creek, Suriname, distributed along 12 km of river (density: one otter per 0.5 kilometres) with a high degree of overlap. Elizabeth Laidler, in the Demerara District of Guyana (a semi-natural environment including irrigation canals), recorded home ranges conservatively estimated at about 32 kilometres of creek or 20 square kilometres of lake (density: one otter per 5.6 kilometres), which may overlap and which encompass core territories with an average size of approximately eight kilometres of creek or five square kilometres of lake. In Yasuní National Park, Ecuador, Victor Utreras found home ranges ranging from 0.5 to 2.8 square kilometres. In the Xixuaú Reserve in the Central Brazilian Amazon, the largest home range was 10.5 kilometres and the smallest was 4.6 kilometres (density: one otter per kilometre) with some overlap. In the Pantanal dry

THE GIANT OTTER

season linear home ranges ranged from 1.1 to 17.8 kilometres (with these extending slightly into flooded areas during the wet season), while exclusive territories varied from 1.1 to 12.7 kilometres (density: one otter per 2.4 kilometres). In general, then, the occurrence of giant otters in their natural environment is characterised by low absolute densities at the landscape level and high local densities in their preferred habitats.

It is evident that food availability, habitat features (water body type and structure), seasonality, level of anthropogenic disturbance, and giant otter density in the area all influence home range and core territory size, as well as the degree of overlap between home ranges, and hence the intensity of conflict between groups. Giant otters have smaller home ranges than expected for a carnivore species of its mass. Territories of terrestrial predators such as jaguars, for example, are larger than those of giant otters by a factor of 150.

SMALL OTTERS, GIANT APPETITES

The group is slow to return to the den, easily distracted by novelties, so Isla swims ahead, sticking close to the shoreline. As she nears the den, she is greeted by her two cubs, about three months old, who have been waiting patiently outside. Together they climb up the bank and enter the den. When they emerge ten minutes later, Isla's teats no longer turgid, they are closely followed by another fully grown otter. Meanwhile, the rest of the family has caught up. The babysitter, Trebol, is hungry and the cubs are excited, so the group does not linger at the den.

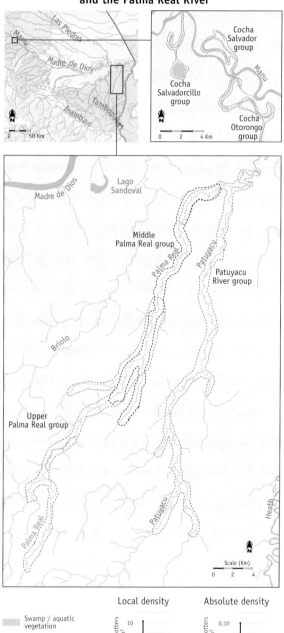

Comparison of giant otter densities and home range sizes of three resident groups in the Manu floodplain and the Palma Real River

Local density: The number of otters per square kilometre of aquatic habitat

Absolute density: The number of otters per square kilometre of total habitat, including forest areas.

The breeding female returns to the den to pick up her cubs who are waiting eagerly outside. (FH)

Trebol is lucky. Soon he catches a small tiger catfish in the shallows and begins to eat it dorsally, almost biting it in half. A sub adult begs him persistently, for about fifteen minutes, before finally being given a small scrap. Another sub adult adopts a different tactic; she is silent but watches carefully and periodically scavenges titbits that fall into the water. The two cubs, meanwhile, being poor swimmers, feel secure only while standing on submerged branches. Isla brings one a bujurki. With fierce, guttural cries and growls and violent blows of his tail, the cub threatens any otter that approaches him. Isla watches him benignly as he settles down to eat the fish. His brother, meanwhile, stands just behind him on the same log and begs with ear-piercing, high-pitched cries. Hueco responds by offering him a small huasaco. The vigorous thrashing of the second cub's tail upsets his balance so that he tumbles into the water and loses his fish.

REPRODUCTION

A resident giant otter group consists of a single, monogamous, reproductive pair and their offspring of several years. The dominant female in each family produces one litter per year and other adults do not breed, suggesting reproductive suppression. We do not yet know if and how this is achieved but inhibitory hormones released through scent-marking may play a role. The breeding female can usually be identified by elongated, turgid teats indicating she has a litter that is still suckling (teats do not return to their original pre-litter shape).

Interestingly, at least three different field studies in Brazil and Guyana have reported the presence of two lactating females, both with the pronounced teats that are typical of nursing mothers, within the same group. However, it was not possible to confirm that the three pairs of females were indeed all nursing cubs. Pseudo pregnancy – in which a female shows all the physical symptoms and behaviours of being pregnant, including the presence of elongated teats and even milk, but later proves not to have been pregnant – has been well documented for giant otters in captivity. There is no reason to suppose that pseudo pregnancy does not occur in the wild and it is tempting to suggest this may be the explanation for the observations of multiple lactating females. Possibly, and Dr. Helen Bateman of the Center for Conservation and Research of Endangered Wildlife (CREW) at the Cincinnati Zoo stresses this is mere speculation, females synchronise their oestrus cycles and therefore ovulate around the same time, but only the dominant female becomes pregnant while the subordinate female, most likely a younger sister or oldest daughter, experiences a pseudo pregnancy or induced lactation. The latter is energy intensive so why would such a system evolve? Perhaps, Bateman suggests, a subordinate female must be ready to take over should the dominant female die. Or she does actually help nurse the young and gains valuable experience in cub rearing in the process. Or perhaps the pseudo pregnancy induces the subordinate female to 'want' to help with the dominant female's cubs and thus avoids competition or the danger of her harming them.

Much of what we do know about giant otter reproductive biology has been derived from captive animals: in July 2011, according to the International Studbook for the species, there were officially 87 living giant otters kept in 28 institutions in South America, North America, and Europe. Giant otters are polyoestrus (coming into heat several times a year) as well as spontaneous ovulators, that is, they will ovulate whether there is an opportunity to breed or not, and regardless of whether a male is present. Copulation usually takes place in the water and the mating period may last for several days. The gestation period is between 64 and 77 days. In captivity it was found that copulation occurs very soon after birth or the loss of a litter, and the female may present delayed implantation or embryonic diapause: mating is observed but the embryos do not implant following fertilization, remaining instead in a state of suspended growth until conditions are more favourable, which may be months later. It is possible that, in the wild, the breeding male in a resident group ensures paternity of the next litter by mating with the female as soon as she has given birth or lost a litter, thereby discouraging sneak matings by transient males.

LITTER TIMING AND SIZE

Giant otters are capable of breeding year-round. In Manu, litters were born in all four quarters of the year, but the number recorded varied between quarters, showing a high degree of seasonality: 68% of litters were born in the second quarter (beginning of the dry season) and 21% in the third quarter (end of the dry season). Only 11% were born during the wet season (first and fourth quarters combined). Thus, the timing of breeding and early stages of cub development in the wild is modified by climatic conditions, with a peak of births in the early dry season coinciding with a peak in abundance and availability of fish. The mother is therefore able to meet her nutritional demands while she is nursing and cubs find it easier to catch their own food when water levels are lower and conditions are more stable.

Although the norm is one litter per group per year, in two different cases we recorded two litters born to the same group within the same year. In Manu, litter size ranged from 1 to 5 with an average size of 2.2 for 78 litters. Every year, several giant otter groups failed to raise litters, so that average reproductive success (the number of cubs produced per group per year, including years when no cubs emerged from the den) was only 1.5. In Xixuaú mean litter size was 1.8 for 12 litters, and in Balbina it was 2.0 for 36 litters.

In captivity, mean litter size was 3.2 for 98 litters. Eight litters of six cubs were reported: as far as I know, this has never been recorded in the wild. Females have four teats and, in captivity, cubs may hold the teat in their mouths even while asleep, hinting at fierce competition among them. This could explain why litters greater than four cubs are rarely observed in the wild, since the weakest will have died in the den.

We watched four groups in Manu move litters of young cubs, estimated at between two weeks and one month old, between dens. Of the 17 cubs involved, 12 were subsequently recorded during the annual census. If typical, this suggests a cub mortality of at least 30% before the age of six months, while juveniles experience a mortality rate of about 37% each year. In the Palma Real watershed, average litter size was 1.3. As in Manu, every year several groups failed to raise litters and so average reproductive success was only 0.6. Of the ten cubs recorded, only four survived to become sub-adults, giving a juvenile mortality of 60%. Although the sample size is small, reproductive success is markedly lower and juvenile mortality significantly higher in the Palma Real than in the Manu area. Scarce data from surveys in other headwater rivers of the region supports this finding.

CUB DEVELOPMENT

At birth, cubs are furred, blind (the eyes open after week four), and already have canines. They spend the first six weeks or so mainly in the seclusion of the den. During this time they may be left in the company of a babysitter while their mother is out hunting and are generally only seen during den changes. The cubs may also be taken out of the den for brief enforced dips in the water as early as two weeks after birth, to learn to swim:

'... After entering the den, Isla brings out a very small cub, which squeaks thinly and frequently. Isla, her teats swollen with milk, grips it by the neck, and brings it to a nearby log, hidden by branches. She growls, threateningly and monotonously, making it clear that the other family members should keep well away from the cub. After a brief moment she takes it back into the den. The cub measures roughly 30 centimetres in total length. All otters have entered the den by 12:15 pm.

'They emerge at 2:15 pm, Isla again bringing out a cub, this time with a belly so full of milk its skin looks tight and it resembles a sausage with legs. She takes it further for a swim, all others showing a careful interest. Isla again growls, briefly. Then she returns it to the den. Hueco and Isla mark the lip of the entrance and the immediate vicinity assiduously.'

Field notes, Cocha Otorongo, 30 October 2001

From about 1.5 months old, cubs can be seen independently entering and playing in the water although they are still carried over larger distances by adult family members. At roughly two months of age, the cubs go on their first hunting excursion with the rest of the group and quickly begin to take an interest in eating solids; soon after,

When cubs are tiny and helpless, time spent outside the den is kept to a minimum. A babysitter, usually an older sibling, often stays with them while the rest of the group hunts. (FH)

they make their first (unsuccessful) attempts at fishing. Cubs can be distinguished from older animals by their slightly lighter coat colour, smaller heads and thinner necks, comparatively larger ears, jerkier movements, inability to periscope, and their tendency to swim lower in the water and in close proximity to each other. As soon as they are accustomed to eating solid food (though lactation continues), the cubs begin to demand or steal fish from their older siblings or their parents, loudly and persistently. Cub begging vocalisations can be heard from a great distance and parents and older siblings eventually respond by offering small prey or pieces of fish.

When they have just captured a prey or immediately after having stolen or been given a fish, young otters utter loud, garbled screams and gurgles, and generally display great excitement. Taking the prey to a partially submerged log, the cub will grip the fish possessively in its jaws, and amidst more loud growls, thrash its tail from side to side, seeking to prevent others from approaching and stealing its prize.

The cubs start to travel around the family home range by about three to four months of age by which time they actively participate in alarm behaviour though not always directed at the perceived threat. By four months, the young almost always participate in group hunting for several hours at a stretch and can catch their own prey. Until then they are dependent on their mother. They are weaned by about five

Above: *A cub's persistent, ear-splitting cries convince a sub adult to share his catch. Begging cubs can be heard from a distance of several hundred metres; this highly conspicuous behaviour often betrays the family's presence on a lake.* (FH)

Right: *Giant otter cubs are vulnerable and mortality is high; at least a third will not survive the first six months.* (ND)

Below: *As youngsters mature, family members become less willing to share.* (RS)

or six months, after which they are referred to as juveniles. At this stage they are still considerably poorer hunters than their parents, but seem to attain adult proficiency by about 10 months. Juveniles begin marking on the group's campsites at between five and 10 months old.

ALLOPARENTING

The giant otter breeds cooperatively. Alloparenting, where individuals other than the parents take on some care of the young, includes providing cubs with fish and teaching of hunting skills by sibling sub-adults and adults of either sex. Alloparents will also rush to the cubs' defence in the face of danger, help carry them or flank the carrying parents during den changes, and, occasionally, babysit them in the den while the mother forages with the rest of the group. Cubs are highly vulnerable: they could conceivably be attacked in the den by snakes such as the bushmaster (*Lachesis muta*) or fer-de-lance (*Bothrops atrox*), small cats like the ocelot (*Leopardus pardalis*) or jaguarundi (*Herpailurus yagouaroundi*), or by a transient giant otter. An incident of infanticide by a male transient was reported in the Brazilian Pantanal during which two cubs fled a den the foreign male had entered and one was pursued, killed, and eaten.

In Cocha Otorongo, Manu National Park, during the first months of life, roughly half the time the group went hunting the cubs were accompanied in the den by a babysitter (occasionally more than one); the other half of the time the cubs were left on their own. Of 37 observations where it was possible to identify the babysitter, only on six occasions did it involve one of the reproductive pair (three times each). The task of babysitting was therefore largely the responsibility of older siblings: the breeding female is not able to stay with the cubs frequently or for long periods if she is to satisfy her own nutritional requirements (regurgitation with the express purpose of feeding another group member, as seen in canids, has never been observed in giant otters). However, babysitting was not witnessed during a study in the Xixuaú Reserve, in the central Brazilian Amazon: this might be explained by differences in predator abundance or level of human disturbance. Also, smaller groups might not be able to afford to leave one of their number with the cubs.

With increasing age, parents and older siblings become less inclined to bring morsels for the cubs and their cries are ignored. The youngsters become more and more frustrated and may resort to snatching fish from their elders. Few prey items are shared in their entirety with cubs, with most larger fish being consumed by adults until only a tail remains, at which point it is directly offered to a begging cub or allowed to be stolen. The pressure to catch their own prey increases, and so does their hunting success. Each capture is announced with cries of triumph and excitement while it is taken to the shore; cubs have difficulty eating their prey 'on the swim'. Begging behaviour is generally observed until the cubs are one year old, but, in the absence of cubs, sub adults will also beg. Very rarely, aging otters will beg too. On two occasions we saw an elderly breeding female beg loudly from her mate; her cries were less high-pitched than a cub's but she exhibited the same excited gargle and tail waving when she was given a fish.

CUB FEEDING

In Manu, giant otters change their diets seasonally, with prey selection shifting from medium and large (more than 20 centimetres) fish in the wet season to a more specialised diet of small (less than 20 centimetre) prey found along lake edges in the dry season. Shallows hunting was also more common when cubs between two and four months old were present. Elke Staib and Lisa Davenport speculate that otters choose different hunting methods in different seasons to accommodate young cubs, specifically their limited swimming abilities and poor handling skills. Though shallows hunting is not the most efficient method in terms of fish capture rate, groups may have an incentive to prey on the small but abundant cichlids in edge habitats because they are ideal baby food and easily handled by young cubs, or because the cubs have access to logs and open edges to rest while adults hunt. A third reason for families with cubs to restrict their foraging to shorelines could be to avoid separation, and hence predation of cubs by caimans. This behavioural and dietary flexibility suggests a high adaptability of otters to different conditions.

Though giant otters give birth to cubs at the beginning of the dry season – from May to September in south-eastern Peru – and this is when the nursing female requires more food, the average time spent hunting was reduced (57%) compared to the wet season (67%), whereas time spent in the den was increased, from 12% in the rainy

A cub's eye view of life in a Colombian river. (FT)

months (from October to April) to 23% in the dry season. In Manu National Park, otters hunted more successfully in the dry season, when catch rates were more than twice that achieved during the wet season (3.8 and 1.8 fish/otter/hour respectively). This is probably due to the greater availability of prey and more favourable hunting conditions during the dry months. Many Neotropical fish species spawn in the rainy season, resulting in a greater number of fish in the early dry season. Moreover, water levels are lower in the dry months, by up to two metres in lakes and several metres in rivers; a larger number of fish in a reduced volume of water leads to a higher density of prey. Furthermore, an increased sedimentation rate results in greater water visibility; giant otters hunt by sight, although their long and abundant facial whiskers also aid prey detection. Prey availability is likely to be the determining factor for cub-rearing during the dry season.

REPRODUCTIVE LIFESPAN AND SKEW

In Manu, average female reproductive lifespan was 5.4 years, with earliest age at first litter being 3 years, although average age at first reproduction was 4.4 years. Litters were, however, produced for an average of only 3.2 years. Each year, therefore, several dominant females failed to raise a litter. Average male reproductive lifespan was 5.2 years, with 3 also being the earliest age at which males sired their first (recorded) litter; average age at first litter was 4.6. Litters were produced for an average of 3.1 years. Thus, male and female giant otters show very similar traits with respect to average ages at first litter (female 4.4 years., male 4.6 years.), average reproductive life-spans (female 5.4 years., male 5.2 years.), and average cub productivity (female 6.9, male 6.7 cubs per lifetime). In a monogamous breeding system, where males experience similar constraints to females, this is not surprising. By way of comparison, in captivity the youngest female at first birth was 2.5 years old but six other females were approximately 3 years old at first birth. The average age of females at first reproduction was 4.3. The youngest captive male to sire a first litter was 2.3 years old, and the average age at first reproduction was 5.5 years.

The reproductive skew was high for both sexes, meaning that only a small proportion of the population were breeders. Of 41 reproductively mature females, 27% were not recorded to produce a single litter, 41% produced only one or two litters, and 32% produced three litters or more. Females that did breed produced, on average, 7 cubs in their entire lifetime. Of 50 reproductively mature males, 38% were not recorded to produce a single litter, 32% produced only one or two litters, and 30% produced three litters or more. Breeding males produced a mean of just under 7 cubs per lifetime. The longest reproductive lifespan was 13 years for males and 11 years for females. The variance in reproductive success thus tended to be higher in males compared to females. The high degree of reproductive skew found in giant otters, comparable to that in other highly cooperative breeders such as the dwarf mongoose

(*Helogale purvula*), the African wild dog (*Lycaon pictus*), and the meerkat (*Suricatta suricata*), means that only 30% of the population consisted of breeding animals.

GROUP SIZE, TERRITORY QUALITY, AND REPRODUCTIVE SUCCESS

As described earlier, giant otters fare better in some habitats, like the Manu floodplain, while apparently living on the edge of survival in others, as seems to be the case in the Palma Real watershed. For example, average resident group size in Manu lakes was 6.0, while the average size of transient groups was 2.9. The largest group numbered 13 individuals. In the Palma Real River, however, a much smaller tributary than the Manu River that does not include lakes, average resident group size was only 3.6, while the average size of transient groups was 2.0. The largest group seen here was only six otters.

In Madre de Dios, there is a strong positive correlation between lake surface area and the intensity of use by giant otters. Less energy is expended when hunting in a home range encompassing a single large lake than if several, smaller water bodies which are spaced some distance apart need to be accessed in order to meet dietary requirements. The advantages could lie in shorter transit times and routes, better demarcation and knowledge of the areas, as well as a smaller radius of activity during cub-rearing. Moreover, there is a statistically significant relationship between giant otter group size and lake size, with larger groups tending to inhabit the largest lakes while territories with the smallest area of lake supported only otter pairs. Mean group size increased by one individual for an increase of approximately 17 hectares of core territory size. In the Pantanal, too, territory size was found to be correlated with group size.

Larger groups also exhibit higher reproductive success, though it was not possible to determine whether a larger number of cubs are born in larger groups or a larger number of cubs died early in smaller groups. Group size plays a role in improved hunting efficiency, better defence against predators, and the ability to hold on to a territory and raise cubs. Moreover, alloparenting helps to increase the survival rate of cubs and juveniles, and hence further increases group size. A study in the Xixuaú Reserve also found a strong positive correlation between group size and reproductive rate. Furthermore, larger groups are more stable: the probability that group size is reduced below a threshold level or that the group disintegrates (for example, following the death of one of the breeding pair), is smaller. Not surprisingly, then, offspring productivity is highest on the largest lakes. In Manu, almost 70% of all cubs are born in only four of the thirteen censused home ranges, each of which included one of the four largest oxbow lakes. In these territories, litters were also larger at emergence from the den. It seems that when a giant otter group can claim the whole of a large lake, they have access to more fish, resulting in a larger group. Though even the smallest territory offers sufficient food security

Family tree for the Cocha Otorongo group-Manu National Park 1988-2005

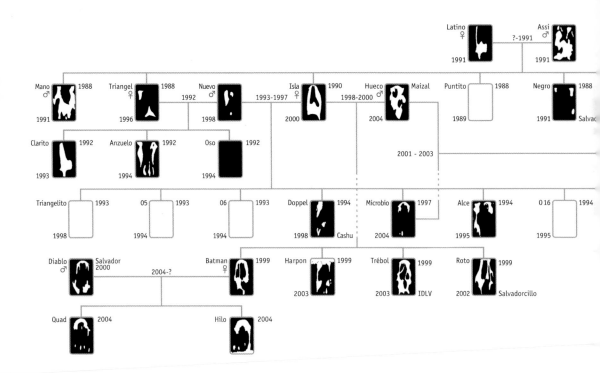

Family tree for the Patuyacu River group-Bahuaja Sonene National Park 1999-2004

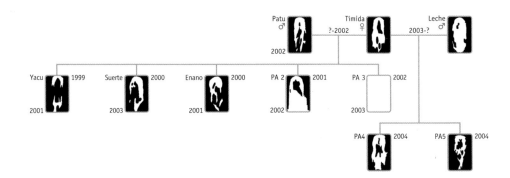

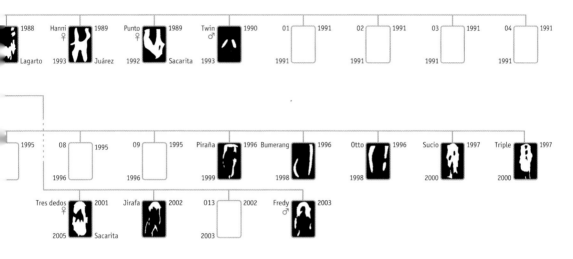

First row (1988–1991):
1988 — Lagarto
Hanni ♀ 1989 / Lagarto 1993
Punto ♀ 1989 / Juárez 1992
Juárez — 1993
Twin ♂ 1990 / Sacarita 1993
Sacarita
01 1991 / 1991
02 1991 / 1991
03 1991 / 1991
04 1991 / 1991

Second row (1995–1997):
1995
08 1995 / 1996
09 1995 / 1996
Piraña 1996 / 1999
Bumerang 1996 / 1998
Otto 1996 / 1998
Sucio 1997 / 2000
Triple 1997 / 2000

Third row (2001–2003):
Tres dedos ♀ 2001 / 2005 Sacarita
Jirafa 2002
013 2002 / 2003
Fredy ♂ 2003

▲
Cocha Otorongo family data

Average group size: 7.5

Average litter size: 2.3

Reproductive success: 2.2

Number or otters reaching: 1.3
sexual maturity per year

Patuyacu river family data

Average group size: 4.8

Average litter size: 1.5

Reproductive success: 1.2

Number of otters reaching: 0.4
sexual maturity per year

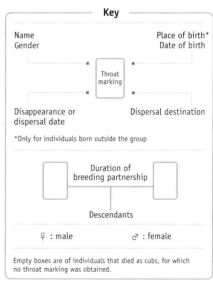

Key

Name | Place of birth*
Gender | Date of birth

Throat marking

Disappearance or dispersal date | Dispersal destination

*Only for individuals born outside the group

Duration of breeding partnership

Descendants

♀ : male   ♂ : female

Empty boxes are of individuals that died as cubs, for which no throat marking was obtained.

As a river erodes its banks, large meanders become isolated over time and oxbow lakes are eventually formed, creating a mosaic of habitats in lowland floodplains. We found that giant otters fare better on these oxbow lakes, shown in the foreground (above, ABT), than they do on small rivers (left, WW).

to support a breeding pair in most years, thereby potentially enabling all breeding females to produce cubs in most years, only where lake size gives groups greater food security, are they able to raise larger litters.

Territory quality is thus an important contributory factor to breeding success. Partner compatibility also plays a role. Reproductive animals usually remained in their home range until death or disappearance. When members of a breeding pair of a similar, young age occupy a high quality territory, they have the potential for high reproductive success: the five most productive breeding pairs we observed produced at least 10, 11, 19, 21, and 25 cubs within their respective territories.

ALLOPARENTING AND REPRODUCTIVE SUCCESS

The number of helpers (non-breeding adults and also sub-adults) was found to be greater in larger territories. The mean number of helpers varied among territories between zero (at one territory none were observed in seven survey years) and 2.6; the maximum observed was five. Does the presence of helpers, likely to be closely related to the dominant pair, contribute to their breeding success? More cubs were indeed born in those territories where, on average, more helpers were present in the birth year. We also found that cubs were more likely to survive to the next (juvenile) year when more helpers were present in the birth year. The mother's need to provide milk during a long weaning period requires her to hunt more intensively than other family members. Mothers also share food at higher rates with young and therefore shoulder the greatest energy burden. It seems that having helpers may facilitate the survival of larger litters than the mother can provide for alone, and as helpers themselves become older, they gain in skill development so that their helping contribution correspondingly increases. In fact, each additional individual helper was associated with an increased probability of cub survival of 42%. The number of helpers present in the juvenile year, however, had an opposite effect on survival rate, with each individual helper decreasing juvenile survival probability by 32%. In other words, it seems that helpers begin to compete with cubs, presumably for food, once the latter are over the age of six months.

Perhaps most interestingly, not only was there a significant positive correlation between the number of dispersers leaving their birth territory and its core area, with the largest territories producing more dispersers, but we also found that cubs produced in larger territories were more likely to disperse successfully at maturity, where we define successful dispersal as either founding a new group or joining an existing one, and producing cubs at least once. Most groups with core territories below 70 hectares produced no successful dispersers over the study period. Again, these findings have important implications for giant otter conservation, as we shall explore in Chapter Five.

A CAIMAN IN THE SHADOWS

As the group continues to hunt in the shallows, it comes across a one and a half metre black caiman, roughly the same length as an adult giant otter. The caiman is lying tail to shore, next to a log. Two giant otters investigate and snort at it briefly. The family then moves on and the caiman swims towards the middle of the lake. Harpon turns back to follow it and the caiman speeds up before submerging. Before long, the group meets a second, larger caiman, more than three metres in length, lying in shallow water. This time, all otters periscope and snort energetically. Five circle it in a half moon and Trebol goes on land behind the caiman, darting forward to mock bite its tail. The caiman splashes dramatically but holds its ground. Most of the otters withdraw, but Isla stands with her forequarters on a log and initiates the high alarm call. Another otter takes up the call, and five or six individuals approach the caiman again. One is a cub which an adult otter grabs by the neck and carries to safety. The caiman lunges in the direction of the others, ending up with part of his body on shore. Satisfied, the otters hum amongst themselves before gradually losing interest and swimming onwards.

NATURAL MORTALITY AND SURVIVORSHIP

Reports of mortality are rare and it has proven difficult to establish whether the giant otter suffers mortality more from accidental or anthropogenic causes, direct predation, conflict with other otters, or other factors: dead animals are almost never found since bodies sink immediately, or they die in the den or in dense vegetation. Decomposition in a tropical environment and predation on dead animals probably play important roles.

We once found the remains of a cub, perhaps two weeks old, near the entrance of a den, but there was no indication of how it had died. As mentioned earlier, a male transient killed and ate a cub of a resident group in the Brazilian Pantanal; infanticide is not uncommon in the Lutrinae in general. We know from demographic data that, in Manu, mortality is highest for young animals – at least 30% before the age of six months, while juveniles experience a mortality rate of about 37% each year – and for dispersing age classes, all of which is almost entirely unexplained. The primary cause of death in giant otter cubs in captivity is parental stress caused by human disturbance, leading to inadequate care.

In the Balbina hydroelectric reservoir in Brazil, two natural deaths, other than the predation of a transient by a jaguar, were recorded. The carcass of a young adult female was found, also at a den entrance, without any visible injury, but in an emaciated condition. The second otter was found by rangers in the water, still breathing but seriously wounded, surrounded by a group of six to eight other giant otters. The rangers pulled the injured otter to the shore where it died shortly after. It had been severely bitten around the snout and genital areas as well as near the forelimbs: such wounds are apparently typical of attacks by other otters.

According to Jorge Schweizer, an encounter in the Brazilian Pantanal between two different groups also resulted in serious injuries to one adult otter as well as the death of a cub. Thus, aggression between groups, or between groups and foreign individuals (intraspecific conflict), though not observed frequently, is potentially an important mortality factor discussed further in Chapter Three.

The giant otter is highly susceptible to parvovirus and distemper which may be transmitted to wild populations by village dogs (see Chapter Four). Transient otters are potential vectors for transmission of these diseases, though this has never been confirmed. Many internal parasites – cestodes and nematodes – have been recorded in the stomach, intestines, heart, and lungs of giant otters and we have frequently observed the tell-tale bumps of botfly larvae developing under the skin. These eventually emerge to pupate and must cause considerable discomfort. However, we have never seen cases of severe botfly infestation and it is unknown how parasites affect fitness and mortality.

Survival to dispersal age in Manu National Park was approximately 50%. Post-independence survivorship differed between the sexes, with a marked pulse in male dispersal at age 3 years, resulting in a lower male survivorship at this time. All males have left their natal groups by age 4.5. Females dispersed as young as one year old but may stay on in their natal territories up to two years longer than males (6.5 years). After a period of high survival during the early adult years (ages 4.5 to 7.5), survival rate declined with age, first gradually and then more rapidly. Females

Botfly larvae, here on the flank of a young, male giant otter, are a common parasite of rainforest mammals. (FH)

show lower mortality than males until roughly eight years old, at which point females begin to show higher mortality, potentially due to the fitness costs of raising multiple litters. Giant otters generally experience low mortality among adult territory-holders. Life expectancy peaks between 4.5 and 5.5 years, with the longest-lived male and female last seen at 15.5 years and at least 13.5 years old, respectively. These are the oldest free ranging giant otters recorded. In captivity, individuals of both sexes may live up to 16 to 20 years.

TIME FOR A SIESTA

By midday, the cubs are weary. Isla leads them to a huge tree that collapsed into the lake several years ago, its branches skeletal in the harsh light. She climbs up a fat limb, and the cubs follow with difficulty, sliding back into the water several times before they manage to get a grip. Tiny long-nosed bats roosting under a patch of loose bark are disturbed into flitting elsewhere for shelter. One by one the rest of the group clambers up the log and begins to bask in the sun. Trebol presses his belly flat against the warm bark and rubs his throat and chin against its roughness, his legs splayed on either side of the trunk. A large, weeping swelling on his haunch betrays the presence of a botfly larva; it is quiet now but at night Trebol is sometimes jarred awake when it bites into his flesh. Harpon, still in the water, grooms himself, nibbling the fur on his flank. Hueco, meanwhile, is companionably grooming Isla who sunbathes with her eyes half shut. Soon all ten otters are out of the water, their fur drying rapidly in the heat. One of the otters makes a small bleating sound, as if in pleasure. Tails, whiskers, and webbed feet twitch

The family interrupts or concludes morning hunting sessions to sunbathe on large, fallen trees. We have observed as many as ten otters out of the water at any one time. (FH)

constantly. A sub adult clambers over the others, and ends up grooming a cub. Suddenly, Isla bolts upright from her resting position on the log and gallops along it straight towards them. The sub adult takes one look at her and dives headlong into the water, uttering a brief, sharp grating sound. No other otter seems to react so extremely to Isla's sudden movement, except to express momentary surprise, and Isla settles down to groom the same cub.

After twenty minutes, one of the sub adults has had enough. She peers over the side of the tree trunk and slowly slithers down it, letting herself drop with a splash into the water. Startled awake, the other youngsters also become restless. Soon, only Isla, Hueco, and the cubs are still on the log; everyone else is waiting in the water. Harpon eventually goes off by himself, and Trebol hums 'Let's go.' Isla pays no attention. Hueco gets up and joins the others. The cubs follow him, their bodies hugging the trunk until they can no longer hold their balance and plop into the water. Finally, Isla yawns, and gives in. Once again, she leads the family towards the den, the group hunting en route but without the intensity of the morning.

TIME BUDGET, HIERARCHY, AND PLAY

Giant otters spend approximately 60% of their day hunting. There is one peak in hunting activity from early- to mid-morning (7:00 to 9:00), and a second, less pronounced peak in the late afternoon (15.00 to 17.00). Groups without cubs showed a more marked and earlier peak in morning hunting activity (6:00 to 8:00). The drop in hunting activity at midday was reduced and a significant decrease did not occur until 17:00.

In Manu, almost 40% of a giant otter day is spent resting in the den, or basking on fallen tree trunks (22%), and in social behaviour involving scent-marking, grooming, and play in or near their campsites (17%). The mutual care of their fur (allogrooming) and body contact between members of a giant otter family during rest is characteristic and plays an important social role in the unity of the group, of the mated pair, and during cub-rearing. After leaving the water, giants will dry themselves by rubbing and rolling thoroughly and energetically against earth or a tree trunk. Fur is nibbled and scratched.

We have never observed serious fights between family members, and hierarchy within a group is not marked in contrast to many other carnivores. Nonetheless, 10 behavioural observations in two lakes where the resident groups have become habituated suggest that rank according to age, and perhaps gender, does influence group dynamics:

'While Agua (a five-year old female) was grooming one cub on a log, Encarna (the breeding female) swam up rapidly and climbed the log in an authoritative manner, immediately reaching towards the cub. Agua lent over the cub and nuzzled Encarna, then opened her mouth, bent her neck, and shook her head from side to side, loosely and rapidly, about six to eight times in what appeared to be a conciliatory gesture. Appeased, Encarna then groomed the cub together with Agua.'

Field notes, Cocha Salvador, 12 September 2002

'At one point, Dedo (the breeding male) was on the latrine in front of the den entrance, when Diablo climbed up. Dedo growled and stood tall, while Diablo hunched submissively underneath him. Diablo is now a large, two and a half year old male.'

Field notes, Cocha Salvador, 15 September 2002

Giant otters spend much of their resting time grooming, both themselves (left, FH) and each other (bottom, JG), thereby strengthening family bonds.

Eight of the ten observations were made while otters were basking and grooming on logs, one incident occurred on a latrine in front of the den, and one in the water following a brief dispute. It seems, therefore, that hierarchy may be expressed particularly during resting periods, when the otters are grooming and sunbathing, although this may also be due to greater ease of identification of the behaviour when out of the water and in a fixed location. The scarce data suggests that males show more submissive behaviour than females, and that the behaviour is always directed at older individuals of the same sex, in particular the breeding pair. Submissive behaviour entailed head wagging, conciliatory nuzzling, and hunching or back-lying. Dominant behaviour took the form of growling, standing tall, and taking over of cub grooming.

We found that the breeding female tended to initiate group activities, for instance, hunting or the changing of the den. During group excursions, the female also tended to swim ahead and was generally more alert during grooming and

After appetites have been satisfied, the giants live up to the otter's playful reputation. Older individuals indulge in headlong chases, prolonged tussles in the shallows, or ambushes from tree trunks, while leaves and twigs are favourite toys for cubs. (Top, JG; bottom, ND; overleaf, FH)

basking sessions. When the group as a whole approached a potential threat, it was not always the breeding female who led it, however. Sub adults and young adults were as likely to express curiosity or alarm, depending on level of experience or individual personality. Since sexual dimorphism is not pronounced in giant otters, there do not appear to be physical reasons that would favour leadership by a single sex.

Giant otters frequently play, alone and with each other, with varying degrees of intensity and at all ages, for anything between a few minutes to over two continuous hours, once the urge to hunt is for the most part satisfied. Play behaviour is often observed just before entering the den in the afternoon. Play objects include twigs, leaves, bark, and small, live fish, while play with other individuals might involve high speed chases along the shoreline, chases up and down logs, grappling in the shallows, and ambushing. Play is widely thought to have an important social function, as well as increase motor coordination and improve perception capacity.

AS BATS FLY LOW OVER THE WATER

The otters have slept for more than an hour in the cool of the den. When they emerge mid afternoon, they hunt briefly and half-heartedly, still replete from the morning's efforts. As they forage along the shoreline, the otters come across an old den. Isla climbs up the bank, neck outstretched, all her senses sharpened for danger. She carefully investigates the entrance, sniffing at the leaf litter. Hueco joins her. Together they fully explore the site, rustling through the leaves and busily checking every corner. While Isla begins to dig at the entrance, Hueco scent marks the old latrine elaborately. Then he follows Isla into the den, only to be met with a spray of sand.

Meanwhile, the rest of the group is occupied with less serious business. While two otters grapple in the water, mock biting each other, another sub adult initiates an impetuous game of 'catch-me-if-you-can'. She runs a short distance along the shore, stops, then looks behind her to see if anyone is chasing her. When a sub adult takes her up on her invitation she dashes off, running at full speed for about twenty metres and then diving recklessly into the water. Soon five otters are involved in the game, hotly pursuing each other back and forth along the bank. One cub, meanwhile, plays quietly with a leaf. He soon tires of this, however, and launches a series of ambushes on the second cub from a submerged branch. Hueco and Isla, attracted by the racket, enter the fray.

Half an hour later, the otters wind down from their exuberant play. Pairs that were tussling in the water begin instead to groom each other. The cubs have already entered the den. A sub adult slowly climbs up on the latrine, defecates, and then disappears inside the den. One by one the others follow. Isla and Hueco are the last to go in, after scent-marking briefly. As the sun sinks behind the tree canopy on the opposite bank, Hueco lies in the den entrance and surveys the lake. One otter is missing from the group. Sometime during the afternoon, Harpon has separated from the family and will spend the night alone.

(FH)

Cocha Cashu's Generations of Giants

Cocha Cashu, July 2015. A horsefly of some sort drones around my head. There's something cloying about the way it flies, almost, but not quite, brushing my skin. I sit still, hoping it will land on my hair so I can swat it into permanent silence. A toucan loops from one side of the lake to a tall tree on the other, its flight stitching across a fleecy sky. Nearby, red-capped cardinals flit among overhanging branches and three hoatzins, the clumsiest of rainforest birds, fuss peevishly at my presence.

I'm sitting in a wooden canoe in the heart of Manu National Park, south-eastern Peru, waiting for the giant otters to emerge from their den. Cocha Cashu is the name of a small cluster of rustic buildings that make up the Biological Research Station for which I work. It is also the name of the oxbow lake on the shore of which the Station nestles: cocha is the Quechua word for lake and Cashu refers to its cashew nut shape. In fact, Cocha Cashu is one of over 30 oxbow lake 'beads' along the string that is the Manu River.

Oxbows are formed – abandoned, really – as a river pinches off its loops over time to follow a shorter, straighter course. Their size is thus determined by the parent river, with which they eventually have little or no connection. Some oxbows become impenetrable swamps, while others evolve into oases for wildlife. Cocha Cashu is one such oasis. Though rubber tappers and loggers navigated the nearby Manu River a century ago, and students of tropical ecology from far-flung countries have made Cashu their home since 1969, the area surrounding the Station is as wild and pristine as any you're likely to find anywhere in the modern world.

As I wait, I listen for the otters as much as I watch for them. They may be giants but otter heads are small and brown, not unlike the colour of the water, and are easily missed. Otters are also noisy, especially when chasing fish. Their loud exhalations after surfacing from a dive are an instant giveaway. And it's these I hear now.

Picking up my binoculars I scan the edge of the aquatic vegetation. There they are. One has a fish in its jaws and the cracking of its skull and bones is audible even at this distance. Soon the family — two adults and two cubs — head in my direction, wholly engrossed in finding and chasing prey. I push the boat from the shore so they don't bump into me. I want them

(JG)

to see me and to come and investigate. Sure enough, they change direction and swim steadily towards me. When the adults periscope, showing their distinctive white throat markings, I'm ready with my camera and take several photos. Later, when I get back to the Station, I should be able to identify them.

The family gradually makes its way to a large tree that has fallen in the water. If I'm lucky, the breeding pair will haul out on the trunk and I will be able to sex them. First a cub climbs up. An adult sniffs the tree and I hold my breath. The otter looks around — I note the shape of its throat marking (large, with three teardrops) — then it clambers up and lies down alongside the cub. But not before I get a clear view of a set of testicles. So this one's the male. Which of course means the other adult is the mother. Now all that remains is to find out who they are.

Back at the Station, my suspicions are confirmed. The reproductive female is an otter named Footsie, born on this same lake in 2011, sole survivor of a late litter. Her mother, Roto, originally from Cocha Otorongo, disappeared the following year aged 13. Footsie and her father, Diablito, remained and no cubs were observed during 2012, 2013 and 2014. But the male I photographed today is not Diablito; he most likely died due to old age, at around 13 years. It's a new male, who we later name Inkani, meaning 'rain' in the local Matsigenka language. Footsie was only able to breed once she'd reached the right age (over 2 years old, though most females have their

The Cocha Cashu Biological Station, Manu National Park, Peru. (JG)

first litter aged three or more), and with the arrival of Inkani (since inbreeding has never been recorded in the wild). This goes some way to explaining the long absence of cubs on the lake. And not only is there once again a family of giant otters on Cocha Cashu, it's also the 12th example of female territory inheritance documented in Manu.

More than two years have passed since I wrote the words above, and the Cashu otter family now numbers nine individuals, including Footsie and Inkani. Cocha Cashu is good otter territory, historically one of the most important in the Manu floodplain in terms of cub productivity. Researchers have been following the life histories of generations of giant otters on this lake for decades. Short-term studies in the early 1980s were succeeded by annual and ongoing censuses conducted by the Frankfurt Zoological Society and by more in-depth research into the behaviour and ecology of the species by Dr. Lisa Davenport and Dr. Christina Mumm, among others.

In 2011, San Diego Zoo Global (SDZG) took over full management of the Station, in partnership with Peru's National Service for Protected Natural Areas, and in May 2017, SDZG and Oxford University's Wildlife Conservation Research Unit launched a major giant otter research and conservation programme, using Cocha Cashu as a main base. Lead researcher, Dr. Adi Barocas, is undertaking

In search of giants. (JG)

a systematic investigation of key factors potentially impacting giant otter populations in south-eastern Peru, including such threats as overfishing and fishermen-otter conflict, domestic animal diseases such as canine distemper and parvovirus, and, most importantly, gold mining and the resulting contamination of fish prey and the aquatic environment by mercury. It is long-term programmes such as this, financially and technically supported by committed and highly experienced organisations, led by skilled and dedicated researchers, and focused on maximizing conservation impact, that are critical for the continued survival of endangered species like the giant otter.

CHAPTER THREE

A Year Alone

OCTOBER: LEAVING HOME

*H*arpon is awake at 5:40 am. Today he will not hunt on the lake. For a while now he has been feeling restless; the urge is upon him to widen his horizons, to find a mate and to raise cubs of his own, in his own territory. It is the end of the dry season, water levels are at their lowest, and fish are at their most accessible. The time has come to leave Cocha Otorongo, and all that is familiar to him. He slips out of the hollow amongst the tree roots where he has spent the night, defecates perfunctorily, and quietly enters the water. As he heads towards the far end of the lake, he sees his family. They are fishing along the shore and are unaware of him. He swims past them quietly and purposefully, and without looking back, enters the stream that will lead him to the Manu River.

Leaving their birth place after reaching sexual maturity is a major step in the lives of many young otters. (JG)

Dispersers, also known as transients or solitaries, are shy and much less vocal than members of family groups. It is easy to miss them during a population survey. (JMR)

TRANSIENT SLEEPING SITES AND LATRINES

Transients are highly discrete, preferring to keep a low profile, and little is known about their use of sleeping sites. It is thought they generally do not construct dens of their own — since dispersers do not stay long in any given area it makes little sense to invest much time and effort into den digging — but may briefly expand natural crevices or holes in banks. They may also seek shelter in the hollow bases of trees, under fallen tree trunks, or in thick vegetation.

The latrines of transient otters, if present at all, are much smaller and more temporary than group campsites, and transients never trample their scat. They may visit the latrines of groups, sometimes leaving a scat that, again, is not trampled. The fact that scat trampling seems to be confined to family groups suggests it probably evolved in social otters to reduce intra-group conflict and enhance bonding by producing a common group odour. The behaviour probably also lets foreign otters know that a family group, and not a transient, is in the vicinity.

FACTORS INFLUENCING DISPERSAL

Dispersal can be defined as movement away from the birth or natal site, with the final objective of breeding successfully. Prospective giant otter dispersers are first seen fishing slightly separate from their natal group, not immediately attempting to

Transient giant otters travel large distances in search of a mate and a territory. (JMR)

catch up when the family moves on, or generally participating less in group hunting activities. Gradually, over a period of several weeks, they stray further afield with greater frequency and for longer periods, at first still returning to the family den at nightfall but later often sleeping alone. Eventually, they stop making any contact with the family, instead maintaining a careful distance and pausing occasionally outside dens and campsites to sniff cautiously while the group is asleep inside or is absent. Finally, the animals leave the natal home range altogether and become true dispersers. In Manu, the shortest detachment period was approximately four weeks, while the longest took more than four months. If the disperser later returns to the natal home range, it behaves as any other unrelated disperser would, avoiding contact with its family.

The factors that influence dispersal are unclear. Separation often, though not always, occurs at the end of the rainy season and the beginning of the dry season which coincides with pregnancy of the breeding female and the birth of a new litter. In Manu, group size at time of separation did not appear to play a role. Aggressive behaviour was never observed nor was any evidence that an otter was being forcibly expelled from the group. Of 54 dispersers observed in Manu, only four (7.4%) dispersed before they were two years old. The majority did so when they were between two and four years of age: the mean dispersal age was 2.5 years, with a marked dispersal pulse of males in the 2.5-3.5 age class. A study analysing the histology and anatomy of giant otter testes found that two-year old male giant otters were already sexually mature,

We came to know this transient well. Named Pepe, he spent much of his time on the Manu River. Not all dispersers are newly mature individuals: some find themselves on their own after losing their mate. (FH)

as indicated by the presence of spermatozoa. Scarce data obtained from animals in captivity suggests that giant otters reach sexual maturity and mate successfully from about 2.5 years onwards. It seems likely, therefore, that becoming sexually mature triggers dispersal, although there may be additional influences.

ROUTES TO BREEDING

Every giant otter is a potential breeder and as each matures, its tendency will be to try to breed. To achieve this, individual otters must find a mate and a territory with sufficient resources. There appear to be three routes for a young adult to becoming a reproductive animal. The first is to leave the birth territory and encounter an otter of the opposite sex with whom to form a new group in an empty territory. The second is to leave the natal group and fill a vacant breeding position in another resident group. The third strategy is to remain in the birth territory and await an opportunity to take over the breeding position from its parent or sibling. This is only possible if in the meantime the parent of the opposite sex has been replaced by an immigrant (since close inbreeding has never been observed).

Our field data indicates that males never become dominant breeders in their natal groups and either establish a new group elsewhere or are recruited into a resident group if they can claim the dominant breeding status. Females breed either if they inherit the dominant position in their natal group or by forming a new breeding group elsewhere. In Manu, a total of 12 females in seven different resident groups were philopatric, that is, they stayed in their natal home range and took over the breeding position from their mother or sister. We did not record a single case of a male taking over the reproductive position from his father and we did not see any cases of giant otters being accepted into a resident group unless it was to fill a breeding position. Becoming an extra breeder within the group was also never observed.

When the reproductive pair, Latino (female) and Assi (male), disappeared from the Otorongo group towards the end of 1991, their positions were occupied by Latino's daughter, five-year old Triangel, and an immigrant male called Nuevo. Isla, the younger sister of Triangel, stayed within the group even after reaching sexual maturity, eventually pairing up with Nuevo, who was not her father (Triangel 'stepped down' after bearing only one litter; she remained within the group for three more years before disappearing). Interestingly, the same pattern was repeated several years later. In 1997 or 1998, a new male called Hueco, from Cocha Maisal, replaced Nuevo and became Isla's partner. In 2000, when she was about 10 years old, Isla failed to produce a litter and 'ceded' her breeding position to her daughter Microbio (but remained within the group for several months as a non-reproductive member until she disappeared aged 11). In the 2004 census, Microbio, too, had disappeared and her sister Batman had become the breeding female in her place, with yet another new male, Diablo, from Cocha Salvador. In other words, between 1991 and 2004, the Otorongo group experienced four breeding female changes, with sisters or daughters taking over the breeding position, and three immigrant males entering the group as new partners. Existing offspring were invariably adopted by the new males and they usually sired their first litter the following dry season.

The mechanisms by which each change occurred could unfortunately not be observed. For instance, it was not possible to establish whether Triangel no longer had cubs as a consequence of having to concede her position to Isla or whether she had lost her reproductive capacity for some reason and Isla could therefore take her place (although this does not seem likely since Triangel was only about five years old when the change occurred). Isla and Triangel continued to live together in apparent harmony. When Microbio took over from Isla, Isla was at least ten years old. Microbio was less than 7.5 years old when Batman took her place. Hueco had his last litter when he was at least 13.5 years old, after which he disappeared from the group.

In captivity, four females gave birth for the last time when they were approximately 11 years old. One 11-year old female developed a uterine infection. Another female first began to miss oestrus cycles when she was 9.5 years old after which she no longer had litters. All these females produced a large number of litters during their lifetimes, indicating healthy reproductive behaviour. Although data is limited, it seems possible that female breeding capability decreases significantly when they are around 10 to 11 years old. In contrast, two males bred successfully in captivity at 19 years of age and we know of one wild male who sired a litter at 15 years. These data suggest that female giant otters may experience a post-reproductive stage in their lives, possibly indicative of menopause, during which they may continue to assist female relatives in raising young.

SEX RATIO, PHILOPATRY, AND MALE IMMIGRANT INTEGRATION

In Manu, not only were males more likely to become dispersers, there appeared to be more males in the system than females. The sex ratio was 1.5 males to 1 female, though the gender was known of only 91 out of a total of 255 different individuals. It is possible, however, that this skew is an artefact of the easier identification of adult males. The teats of adult females who have not yet raised a litter are very small: these females are not easily distinguished from sub adult males. To discount this, we calculated the sex ratio for 15 litters where the sex was known of all cubs and found it to be 2.1 males to 1 female. Interestingly, a study in the Brazilian Pantanal also found a male-biased sex ratio (1.5:1). When field data is compared with that reported for animals in captivity, we find that in 36 captive-born litters where the sex was known of every cub, 56 cubs were male and 35 were female, giving a ratio of 1.6 to 1.

Although both male and female giant otters disperse, our data indicates that males are the more dispersive sex while females may be philopatric, spending their lives in the home range where they were born. It is possible that the higher level of philopatry in females forces them to compete with each other for access to resources, while males compete primarily with unrelated individuals in non-natal groups. It has been suggested that under such circumstances competition among females could be reduced if females skewed the sex ratio of their offspring in favour of males. It will be interesting to see if data from other wild giant otter populations corroborate our observations.

In the 12 instances (in seven different groups) when vacancies arose for a reproductively dominant female, it was a subordinate female otter – either a sister, or a daughter from the oldest cohort – that assumed dominance. Where more than one subordinate female was present in the oldest cohort, we could not determine the factor(s) that influenced which of the siblings became dominant.

In those same 12 instances, a breeding male disappeared and was replaced by an immigrant adult male. Any cubs of the original pair were adopted by the immigrant males – we did not record infanticide – and groups were stable throughout the transitions, usually producing new litters the following year. In each case, it was not possible to determine whether the replaced male died due to natural causes, was evicted, or was killed by the immigrant male. Original group males were never seen again, but serious fights between individuals were also never observed. Since inbreeding was never recorded, it is when the breeding male of a resident group is replaced by an immigrant male that competition for the reproductive position could potentially arise between his mate and her sisters or daughters.

'SHOULD I STAY OR SHOULD I GO?'

Young adults must weigh the advantages and disadvantages of remaining within their natal family as helpers, thus foregoing their own reproduction, versus attempting successfully to establish groups and raising cubs of their own elsewhere. Initially, both sexes may benefit from staying in the territory of their birth, enjoying improved localisation and exploitation of food resources, better protection against predators, and the familiarity of their home range. Young adults can hone their skills while helping, and take advantage of the accumulated knowledge of older members of the group. By assisting the reproductive pair with the raising of cubs, they are furthering half (in the case of full siblings) or a quarter (in the case of half brothers or sisters) their own genetic information.

A female may have to bide her time for several years, during which she cannot produce litters due to reproductive suppression, before a breeding opportunity arises within the group (and provided her father is no longer the breeding male). Alternatively, she may recognise that resources in her birth territory are limited and her parents therefore less tolerant of helpers, especially if they do not sufficiently offset the cost of sharing those resources. There may also be a low likelihood of acquiring the breeding position. In such circumstances, she might be better off opting for early dispersal in search of better reproductive opportunities.

On the other hand, dispersal carries with it increased risk of serious injury or death, since chances of detecting a predator are smaller, and the odds of finding an empty territory or a vacant breeding position in another group may be slim. We also found that dispersing females that are successful in forming new groups experience a delay in age at first reproduction, decreasing lifetime reproductive success significantly. The average age at which philopatric females were first recorded with a litter was 3.9, compared to an average age of 5.3 years for dispersing females.

If instead she potentially stands to gain the reproductive position in a high-quality home range, the rewards may be well worth the wait. The six territories in Manu where female take-over of the breeding position from their mothers or sisters was confirmed included four where reproductive success was consistently highest. Gaining the right to acquire the natal territory is therefore a significant benefit of philopatry, in addition to the acquisition of skills through helping. Males, however, must disperse eventually if they are to raise their own cubs. Of the dispersers of which we knew their sex, 54% of males and 42% of females succeeded in producing a first litter post dispersal. Although the sample size is small, in Manu dispersing males are thus 29% more likely to reproduce successfully than dispersing females, favouring philopatry in females.

DECEMBER: LEARNING TO SURVIVE

The rainy season has started. The resident family of Cocha Salvador is fishing along the shore when Harpon passes by, swimming in the middle of the lake. One member of the group catches sight of him and the family reacts excitedly, sounding the alarm and periscoping in his direction.

An otter detaches itself from the group and swims rapidly towards Harpon, but in utter silence, apparently intent on scaring off the intruder. Harpon speeds up slightly and the group member, after approaching to within thirty metres, returns to the shore.

Later, Harpon briefly shadows the hunting group, observing them from a distance of one hundred metres or so. He then starts to fish, porpoising in mid-lake, and catches a large boca chico, which he carries to the shore opposite the group to eat. While occupied, a two and a half metre black caiman approaches from behind a log and lunges at Harpon, to steal the fish rather than attack the otter. Harpon manages to jump away with the half-eaten fish, but leaves a few remnants which the caiman snaps up. The otter moves off to finish his prey, returning five minutes later. He circles the caiman, gradually drawing closer and closer, while snorting and periscoping repeatedly. The caiman starts to hiss and raises its body out of the water, posturing in an attempt to intimidate, but when the otter finally approaches to within one metre the caiman beats a hasty retreat. Harpon continues fishing, satisfied his point has been made.

TRANSIENT HUNTING SUCCESS

Dispersers had a lower fish capture rate (2.4 fish per hour) than individuals who hunted in a group (3.8 fish per otter per hour) and therefore compensated by hunting for longer periods. Moreover, several studies found that transients catch smaller fish than do family groups, within a relatively narrow spectrum of species, though the

Harpon finishes his fish while keeping a wary eye on the black caiman. Later, he makes sure the caiman learns who is boss. (RS)

Although giant otters normally consume their prey immediately, they sometimes return to a large prize hours, or even a day, later. (FH)

most important species taken — cichlids and *Hoplias malabaricus* — are the same. One explanation may be that transients, not having a territory of their own and generally avoiding hunting in the exclusive areas of resident groups, are therefore forced to procure their food in sub-optimal fishing areas.

Often dispersers find themselves in unfamiliar terrain so do not know where the best fishing spots are. Driven by the urge to reproduce, dispersers tend to spend more time on the move, stopping only a few days, if at all, in any one location, and depending more on rivers as a hunting zone, where visibility is reduced and where current influences energy expenditure. One aging disperser we met several times on the Manu River seemed to specialise in capturing a large species of armoured catfish (*Pterodoras granulosis*), locally known as a *piro*:

'11:30 am. We find Pepe with a gigantic piro just below Cocha Otorongo. The fish must weigh between ten and fifteen kilograms. Pepe disappears when we approach with the boat. At about 1:30 pm we see him again in the water near the fish. He then sunbathes for about two hours, occasionally cooling off in the water and once checking on his kill. He resumes eating it at around 4:00 pm, during which time he also reflexively catches and devours a small catfish which comes to scavenge. Finally, he swims off into the river, heading upstream.'

Field notes, Manu River, 12 October 2001

COMPETITION

The black, white, and yacare caimans are potentially important competitors for fish. Densities of black caimans are high in the Manu lakes; night counts on Cocha Salvador, for instance, arrived at a total of 344 animals, while densities on most oxbow lakes ranged between one and five caimans per hundred metres of shoreline. However, direct competition for food is generally avoided since caimans are solitary night hunters that ambush their prey rather than actively chase them in groups during the day. As the breeding seasons of both caimans and giant otters coincide, it is possible that competition for prime shoreline denning and nesting sites leads to frequent confrontations on lakes where the black caiman occurs at high densities.

The Neotropical otter (*Lontra longicaudis*), a smaller relative of the giant otter, is much shyer, making comparisons between the two species difficult: no long-term study into Neotropical otter biology and ecology has as yet been carried out in Peru. It is generally believed that competition between the giant otter and the Neotropical otter is avoided due to differences in preferred habitats, periods of activity, and dietary requirements. While giants live in groups and fish together, the Neotropical otter is a solitary hunter. The Neotropical otter is generally assumed to be crepuscular — that is, active at dusk and dawn — and/or nocturnal in habit. However, in remote, undisturbed areas we have found the species to be active at all times of the day. Studies in other countries have shown that Neotropical otters eat smaller fish

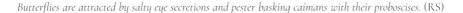

Butterflies are attracted by salty eye secretions and pester basking caimans with their proboscises. (RS)

The Neotropical otter (Lontra longicaudis) lacks the distinctive throat marking and flattened tail of its larger relative... (FH)

... and is often found at much higher, colder altitudes. (FH)

and that they may supplement their piscivorous diet with crustaceans, amphibians, molluscs, small mammals, and reptiles. In the Palma Real, we found that fish species overlap between giant otter and Neotropical otter diets is substantial but that the latter indeed tends to consist of smaller fish. Observations of tracks showed that both species visit each other's dens and marking areas, possibly suggesting interspecific signalling of the use of resources.

The Neotropical otter and the giant otter have similar distribution ranges but the Neotropical otter uses a more varied mosaic of habitats. Neotropical otters have been observed at altitudes above 3,000 metres, while giant otters are usually not seen over 600 metres above sea level. And while the giant otter frequents both still and running waters, in Madre de Dios at least, the Neotropical otter shows a marked preference for streams and rivers. We have only once seen the smaller otter species on an oxbow lake. The absence of Neotropical otters on lakes could be due to the threat posed by black caimans. A caiman will approach a single giant otter if only to steal its prey. The solitary Neotropical otter is presumably more vulnerable on the caiman-dense lakes compared to the smaller streams and rivers where large black or white caimans are rare and where only the dwarf caiman (*Paleosuchus trigonatus*) sometimes occurs.

Neotropical otters might also be avoiding the giant otter groups on lakes. We once witnessed an encounter between a pair of giant otters and a Neotropical otter on the Palma Real River. As they approached each other while swimming, the Neotropical otter spotted the giants, dashed up the river bank a short distance, and stopped to watch them. It stood there quietly for about ten seconds as the giant otters passed by, then ran back into the water and continued downriver. The giant otters simply ignored it as they swam upriver. Although there seems to be a high level of niche separation, it would be interesting to explore the relationship between the two species further.

FEBRUARY: HEADING INTO THE UNKNOWN

Four difficult months have passed since Harpon left his birth lake and his family. The wet season floods have arrived and he avoids the swollen, sediment-laden Manu River, preferring instead the more transparent and still waters of the crescent-shaped oxbow lakes. Some of these abandoned river meanders became isolated from the Manu many decades ago and are choked with semi-aquatic vegetation, gradually being reabsorbed into the forest. Others are young and experience ebbs and floods with changes in the water level of the river, to which they are still connected. Harpon ranges from one to another, passing through in a matter of hours or lingering two or three days in those where fish are plentiful. Twice he enters an aguajal, a swamp dominated by Mauritia palm trees and studded with small, black-as-night pools. He also sees a jaguar for the first time in his life. But nowhere does he meet another lone otter.

Another month later finds Harpon on the Manu River, near the confluence with the mighty Madre de Dios. He has weathered several floods and has even witnessed the inundation of forest surrounding the lakes. He has lost weight and is tempted to return to Cocha Otorongo for a

(JG)

THE GIANT OTTER

(WW)

brief respite, but feels compelled to continue in his search for a mate. Now he hesitates before plunging into the turbid waters of the Madre de Dios. His ears are filled with the clacking sound of large stones rolling over the river bed and the opposite bank is so far away he cannot even see it. Unaware that he has just left the protection of Manu National Park, Harpon lets himself be carried downriver by the swift current.

DISPERSAL DISTANCES

We identified a total of 54 dispersers in Manu. The mean observed dispersal distance was 57.2 kilometres. Forty individuals (72%) were sexed (28 males, 12 females). Males dispersed 65.4 kilometres on average, compared with a mean of 37 kilometres for females; males therefore tended to disperse almost twice as far as females. The findings of a genetics study in the Brazilian Pantanal also suggested a similarly marked difference in dispersal distance between sexes.

In our study, the longest minimum dispersal distance recorded was 148 kilometres. It is likely that some otters dispersed even further, leaving the census area. One male, known as Mano, born in 1988 in Cocha Otorongo and first seen as a disperser in March 1991, was observed in April near the confluence of the Manu and Madre de Dios Rivers, approximately 98 kilometres downriver from Otorongo. In September, Mano was again seen on Otorongo where he avoided the group to which he had belonged.

Thereafter, he was not seen again. Between March and September, Mano therefore covered a minimum total distance of 196 kilometres. Another male, Dedo, born in Cocha Cashu in 1991, disappeared for five years before being seen once more, this time in Cocha Salvador, about 60 river kilometres from his birth lake. Unfortunately, we have no idea how far he wandered during this period. Dedo eventually became the most successful male in Manu, producing at least 25 offspring over his 15-year lifetime.

In 2004, a member of our team carried out a survey of the giant otter population on the Los Amigos River, adjacent and to the north of Manu National Park. In 2007, during the annual census, the Frankfurt Zoological Society noted the presence of a new breeding male on Cocha Salvador in Manu. Incredibly, this male turned out to be one of the otters filmed on the Los Amigos River three years previously, in what is the first documented case of a giant otter moving between two watersheds, involving a minimum estimated distance of about 270 kilometres.

APRIL: STRANGE PLACES, STRANGE OTTERS

Harpon is grooming himself while resting on a partially submerged log when a familiar, strong smell meets his nostrils. He looks intently up into the forest. He is in a stream, only twenty metres or so wide; its high banks and the dense tree canopy overhead make it difficult for him to see clearly. An electric blue morpho butterfly winks past him. Again that smell. Harpon slips into the water and cautiously follows the aroma upstream, sticking close to the bank and keeping his head low. He knows the giant otter family might be around but the temptation to investigate is irresistible.

Otters also groom to keep their fur waterproof and parasite-free. (FH)

He can see the campsite now. It's on a small sandy peninsula at the mouth of a tributary. There is no sign of a den. More importantly, there is no sign of movement so Harpon decides to take a closer look. Numerous tracks are bunched near the water's edge but they are not fresh; the river level has gone down slightly since the otters last visited. Maybe two days ago. Harpon relaxes and climbs up the bank. Once at the top he eagerly sniffs the substrate and the few tiny saplings that survived the otter family's mauling. He strategically deposits his own scat in the middle of the latrine, and deliberately avoids trampling it. Harpon has learned much, but does not want to linger in case the otter pair, with their two offspring, returns.

DISPERSER MATE SELECTION

Dispersing giant otters are not known to establish their own campsites, but may visit those of groups. When a reproductive animal disappears (probably dies), the open position is occupied within a few weeks or months by a disperser. This process generally takes place more quickly than the (re)colonisation of a lake, which might take several years. It is probable that campsites divulge important information to dispersers passing through the home ranges of resident groups, revealing the number, age, gender, and sexual status of members. Dispersers are thus able to evaluate their chances of integration within a group.

In her study area in Guyana, Laidler observed transients – which she assumed to be mostly males – following family groups. The transients regularly shadowed the families into their exclusive areas around the resident juveniles' first birthday, which was also the age at which these juveniles were found to start marking on their parents' campsites. The transients maintained a discrete distance by arriving a day or two after the families had left the area and sometimes deposited scats on the family latrines. Laidler speculated, firstly, that juveniles begin to scent-mark on the family campsites at about one year old in order to reduce parental tension and aggression against them as they matured, and secondly, that the behaviour of transients at this time indicated a mating interest in one or more of each family's juveniles and not a contest for the territories themselves.

There are several possible survival advantages, both for the transient and for the parents and female juveniles in this family-monitoring form of mate selection. The long period of time over which olfactory information is exchanged may mean that both the transient and the juvenile can properly assess each other's reproductive fitness, particularly important in a monogamous mating system where partners pair for a number of years or for life. Also, by reducing the time they are on their own (after dispersal in the female's case), both the resident young female and the male transient may benefit from the possible anti-predator protection that comes with being a mated pair. In fact, Laidler suggests that families may actually tolerate the presence of transients, at least during the resident juveniles' second year of life as they approach sexual maturity.

JUNE: MAKING FRIENDS

It is the start of the dry season and the Madre de Dios River flows clear and serenely treacherous. After tentatively exploring a couple of its smaller tributaries, and only just surviving an encounter with hunters and two dogs, the badly frightened Harpon has tentatively worked his way back upstream until he finally approaches the town of Boca Manu. He decides to skirt it by hugging the opposite bank and then quickly traverses the river to enter the sluggish Manu. Now he feels safer. He intends to return to his birth lake, but he is in no rush. The days pass and his travels are largely uneventful. A pair of capybaras resting on the river bank take him momentarily by surprise and several times he hears a jaguar grunting. Wide, sandy beaches lie exposed and the river, now confined, is choked with fallen trees and woody debris, providing ideal resting sites. One late afternoon, he captures a large catfish. Dusk falls before he can finish eating it, so he pulls it out of the water onto a log, and returns to it the next morning. He is in luck; nobody has stolen his prize overnight. With his belly full, he can afford to take it easy for a while. As he zigzags slowly upriver, he sees a pair of otters ahead on a fallen tree. Harpon eyes them carefully. Will they be friendly?

A dispersing otter may meet a wide variety of other wildlife during its travels, like these capybaras. (JG)

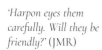

'Harpon eyes them carefully. Will they be friendly?' (JMR)

The confluence of the Madre de Dios and Manu Rivers. (WW)

TRANSIENT GROUPS

When a young adult elects to leave the natal group and to embark on a search for a mate and an unoccupied home range, it takes on a difficult task. In the first 16 years of the Frankfurt Zoological Society giant otter project, only 11 known dispersers were seen to form new breeding groups. Of these, one pair subsequently split up after the death of their first litter; the male formed a new pair with another disperser, Doble (hence the odd number), while the first female disappeared. Following is Doble's story.

Doble was a sub adult when she was filmed by the BBC in December 1998 on Cocha Salvador. We first saw her in May 1999 still participating in family activities. By October the same year she had become a disperser, living on Salvador without associating with her family. When we next saw her in May 2000, still on Salvador, she was together with two other females, Gollum and Puente, both her sisters from different litters. Thus, for a while, Salvador was inhabited by two related groups, one the resident family and the other of dispersers. In October 2000, we found Doble on the Manu River, together with her sister Gollum, and in the company of a male called Pepe. Puente had disappeared. In February and October 2001 we observed Pepe and Doble on the river; by this time she had become very nervous of motorised traffic. Gollum probably died, having dispersed from her natal group at an unusually young age of less than one and a half years. A year later, when Doble was about five years old, we saw her in Cocha Juarez with a different male from Cocha Cashu; they had two cubs. As far as we are aware, this was her first litter. In October 2003, she was again seen on Cocha Juarez, this time alone. Finally, during censuses in October 2004 and September 2005, we found Doble together with two immigrant male otters in Cocha Sacarita.

A giant otter population is typically described as consisting of family groups and of lone dispersers of both sexes. However, our study in Manu confirmed for the first time the existence also of transient groups; loose single- or mixed-sex associations of multiple non-breeding otters (two to five observed, with a mean of 2.9 individuals) that have not yet secured a territory and do not exhibit strong site fidelity. A study into the degree of genetic relatedness among and between individuals from different giant otter groups in the Pantanal supported our findings. It, too, found that the average relatedness within groups was high, as expected, but that some groups were formed by unrelated individuals. Not only that; in two cases, subordinate animals were closely related to each other, but less so to the breeding pair, suggesting that the kin composition of groups may be more variable and the social system of the giant otter more complex than previously supposed. The existence of groups composed of unrelated members also suggests that kin selection alone is not enough to explain the evolution of giant otter sociality.

Reasons for dispersers to associate with same-sex otters or in mixed-sex groups could include benefiting from increased hunting success, reducing the risks of

Transients sometimes team up to form loose associations that may be misidentified by researchers as family groups. (ND)

Lone dispersers have a lower fish capture rate than individual members of a group. (JG)

predation, and increasing the chances of being able to displace a resident group from its home range, or of ousting a member of the reproductive pair of a resident group (if this is indeed what happens). However, in the latter two cases, a question remains regarding the fate of the remaining members of the transient group, since we never witnessed the recruitment of more than one individual into a resident group, nor did we observe a new breeding group being formed by more than two (oppositely-sexed) dispersers. Clearly, there are many exciting questions yet to be answered regarding the ecology of giant otter dispersal.

The following example of Cocha Salvadorcillo illustrates why we believe transient groups to be temporary, dynamic associations of dispersers. In October 1999, a resident family of four individuals was living in Cocha Salvadorcillo. In May 2000, we observed an individual named Paniro, originally from Cocha Maisal, alone on the lake. The following October we again found the family, this time consisting of six members, including three cubs. A year later, in 2001, the resident family numbered five individuals. We failed to find it in September 2002, but were surprised to see Paniro again, this time with two other otters one of which we recognised as being Roto, born in 1999 in Cocha Otorongo; the other was an immigrant to the census area. In the October 2003 census, we encountered not only the resident family, now comprising seven individuals, but also, several weeks later while the group was absent, Paniro and Roto, this time together with a dispersing male called Diablo from Cocha Salvador. As we were filming the group of three, a fourth individual, Chupe, briefly joined them but was subsequently seen hunting alone on several occasions while inhabiting the lake simultaneously with the group of dispersers. In October 2004, we encountered only the resident family in Cocha Salvadorcillo but found Diablo as the breeding male in Cocha Otorongo. A year later, in August 2005, Chupe had become the breeding male in the Salvadorcillo family and Roto had joined another transient group of three otters in Cocha Cashu. There was no sign of Paniro. Thus, during the period between 1999 and 2005, the resident family on Salvadorcillo produced at least four litters of cubs, whereas the transient group was never seen with cubs. Interestingly, the transient group used the dens, campsites, and hunting grounds of the resident family while the latter was absent. In Cashu, Davenport, too, found a transient group usurping the resident family territory during their absences. Transient groups may become resident groups when an opportunity arises, perhaps shedding excess (subordinate) members and establishing a single breeding pair.

Having found a partner and a free territory, the next challenge is the rearing of a first litter of cubs and ensuring their survival to sub adulthood. Average litter size for new breeding pairs in Manu was 1.4 cubs, well below the 2.2 population average. Of the seven new groups formed in Manu only four survived to produce a second litter of cubs. These four groups then went on to persist for at least another six years each, suggesting that once a group has managed to raise two litters its chances of persistence

The future is uncertain for a newly-formed pair of giant otters. Will they succeed in holding their territory and in raising a first litter of cubs? (FH)

are considerably higher. With each litter of cubs, a reproductive pair gains experience and improves cub-rearing techniques. As the family grows the breeding pair benefits from the assistance provided by their older offspring, in terms of babysitting, defence, and feeding of cubs.

SOCIALITY AND TERRITORY DEFENCE

Why did giant otters evolve to live in groups? This is a complex question: how do we disentangle the factor(s) that drive sociality from those that are incidental benefits of group living? It is likely there is no single or simple answer.

Several authors have suggested that living in larger groups may help all family members benefit from the ability to detect or defend against predators like the black caiman or jaguar. Yet, while encounters with these predators, especially caimans, may be frequent, they do not often escalate into a full blown fight and rarely seem to end in deaths of either otters or predators. In fact, there is only one confirmed record of an otter being killed by a jaguar and none by a caiman. While group-living clearly provides enhanced protection against predators, the latter would not appear to be the driving force behind it.

Perhaps giant otters are social to increase prey size or hunting efficiency: shoaling and mobile fish are difficult to capture and individual otters catch more fish when they hunt together as a group. However, giant otters feed mostly on small prey and there is no concrete evidence that members of a group actively cooperate while fishing.

What about cooperative breeding, could that be a factor determining giant otter sociality? Certainly, as discussed in Chapter Two, the presence of helpers to assist with the rearing of cubs brings indirect and direct benefits for both helpers as well as parents.

Philopatry and the inheritance of territories by replacing a dominant individual is also thought to be one of the factors promoting group-living in mammals. However, I suspect the most important factor driving giant otter group living, and one which also provides justification for living with genetically unrelated individuals, is probably linked to the need to protect or acquire a high-quality breeding territory (where quality is defined in terms of the resources a territory provides, primarily food).

As mentioned previously, within groups giant otters are cohesive and cooperative. Aggression between giant otter groups is also rare and appears to be largely avoided through scent-marking. In fact, in some areas, a researcher could spend many months studying giant otters and never witness a violent encounter. It would be natural to assume, then, that giant otters are remarkably peaceable animals, unusually so for such a social carnivore. The combined reports from studies in various parts of the

Discussing drivers and benefits of giant otter sociality is a bit like the timeless question of: Which came first? The chicken or the egg? (FH)

giant otter's distribution range present a somewhat different picture, however, one that suggests the main threat to a group of giant otters appears to be adjacent groups, sometimes resulting in the deaths of adults or cubs, in disputes over territory.

In south-eastern Peru, groups were generally not observed to abandon their home ranges or trespass on others. On the few occasions when a new otter group replaced an existing group, the new inhabitants of the area adopted the same home range, and used many of the same dens and campsites, as their predecessors. Once, however, we did observe a direct confrontation between two groups:

'The resident group of four otters was hunting in deep water when, from the opposite end of the lake, a family of seven individuals appeared, consisting of four adults and three cubs. It was the group observed on neighbouring Cocha Caracol the year before. The two groups swam towards each other, slowly but without hesitating. It was not clear at what point they became aware of each other, but when they were about 20 metres apart, both groups began caterwauling, and raced towards each other, surfing on the surface of the water at great speed. The groups clashed, and a fight ensued. The cubs, estimated to be between four and five months old, joined in the melee. In the confusion that followed, and because we were observing this from a distance of about 200 metres, it was impossible to follow the behaviour of individuals. At times it seemed as though various otters were chasing one animal. Several escaped into the forest and were no longer followed. This all lasted less than two minutes. One family began to re-group and we again counted seven otters. They milled around in the same spot for about five minutes, presumably looking for members of the other group. The family then began to fish, and after about ten minutes swam in our direction. At roughly 30 metres from our vantage point, they all came out onto a log; we could not see any obvious injuries resulting from the encounter. The cubs and adults then continued hunting.'

Field notes, Cocha Endarra, 14 August 2005

Giant otters are highly territorial and a group will actively defend its territory. Serious fights may therefore occur between groups at territory borders or in areas with territorial overlap, especially during the dry season, or when a group tries to establish a new territory or take over an existing one. In the southern Pantanal, a family comprising a mated pair, two adult females, one young male, and six cubs was seen to expel a smaller group of a breeding pair plus two adult females. Another aggressive encounter between two giant otter groups on the border between their home ranges was witnessed in 2003, again in the Pantanal. Four giant otters vigorously pursued a single individual, though two others were in the vicinity of the five participants. The aggressors moved at great speed, literally surfing on the surface of the water, each creating a bow wave and producing a chorus of roars and piercing whistles never heard previously. The group managed to surround the single otter and proceeded to attack it, but it escaped moments later and was persecuted for a further kilometre before the chase was abandoned.

It seems likely, therefore, that group size matters significantly in territory defence: the larger the group, the more easily it can ward off attempted take-over of a breeding territory or acquire one of its own. Interestingly, following one of these confrontations, the resident group vigorously scent-marked the location where the conflict started, strongly suggesting that scent-marking is indeed critical in the establishment and defence of giant otter territories.

On Cocha Cashu, in Manu National Park, prior to taking their three-month cubs on their first hunting forays, I watched the resident otter family patrol the lakeshore of their entire core territory daily, for three consecutive days, with several or all members caterwauling in a chorus, apparently warning unseen neighbours or potential intruders to keep away, and probably providing information on the group's identity, size, composition, and strength, as well as their willingness to fight.

Observations at Karanambu Ranch, in Guyana, confirm that giants are capable of fatal intraspecific aggression. Five otters that were successfully hand reared and returned to the wild were killed by wild giant otters in three separate incidents. On one occasion, three cubs were killed by wild otters in the river, each with a single bite to the skull. One cub was killed immediately upon arrival by a non-rehabilitated male otter; this four-year old individual was later killed by wild otters as he started to range further afield.

AUGUST

Almost a year after leaving Cocha Otorongo, Harpon is back on his birth lake. He has seen his family, but is content to observe them from a distance. It is good to be in familiar terrain once more. Harpon spends several days on the lake, visiting the old haunts when the group is elsewhere. But soon he becomes restless again and he extends his daily forays to include other lakes. Once he meets a solitary male in Cocha Salvadorcillo but steers clear of him. Every lake he investigates is already occupied by a group of otters. There is no future for him here and Harpon decides to leave the Manu floodplain and instead explore a tributary deep into the forest.

Worlds Apart

The otter changes course and heads into a crystalline, shallow tributary. I snatch up my binoculars and see it flush a large catfish, water surging as it chases its prey over a sand bank. The fish escapes and the otter, too, is swallowed by the jungle. How will we identify it now?

'Quick, let's follow on foot,' I say to Frank. 'We might be able to catch up.'

Frank gestures to our boat driver, Zacarias, to nudge the bow of our fifteen-metre canoe into the mouth of the stream. I grab the day's provisions and tug on a pair of light trainers, token protection against sting rays. Then I swing my legs over the side and lower myself into the current, enjoying the shock of cool water on my skin. Frank follows, the camera and zoom lens slung around his neck. Zacarias reverses the engine; he agrees to moor the boat nearby and wait for us.

It is mid-morning. The sun is a hot weight on our shoulders and leaches the green from the surrounding vegetation. We are nearing the end of our annual giant otter census in Peru's Manu National Park. We have already filmed all the resident families, but the nomadic solitaries present a greater challenge. They are elusive, silent, and secretive.

I push my feet through the water, feeling the thin cotton of my trousers swirl against my legs. Pristine, crescent-shaped beaches flank the banks of the meandering stream. Water slips sinuously between rocky shelves and over drifts of sand, nibbling at miniature, sculpted cliffs until they crumble and dissolve. The polished trunk of a majestic ceiba spans the current, its bark long gone, its sun-warmed wood smooth and satisfying to the touch. I revel in the freedom of walking in the stream, after so many hours spent in the dense, claustrophobic forest.

There is surprisingly little wildlife. No sign of the otter, only small schools of fish flitting from pool to pool. I disturb a sting ray, a tiny spurt of sand staining the water where it had been resting. Lime and lemon butterflies shiver on damp soil where a tapir urinated at dawn. Twice I spot the tracks of capybara. I know it is the wrong time of day for animals to be out and about, yet I am disappointed.

Sand bunches in my socks, rubbing raw the skin between my toes, and the vicious sting of a horsefly enhances my discomfort. By now, I have given up hope of seeing the

'Lime and lemon butterflies shivered on damp sand.' (WW)

solitary otter again. A shady spot on a beach tempts me and I whistle to catch Frank's attention.

'Let's stop awhile, have something to eat,' I call to him. The sound of my voice makes me wince. Like shouting in a cathedral or an ancient library, it seems wrong, irreverent.

Frank flops down next to me. 'I feel like Alfred Russell Wallace,' he says, looking at our tracks on the sandy canvas. 'Like we're the only humans ever to have ventured here.'

I nod. A kingfisher arrows past, it's challenging chatter ringing in my ears. I push myself off the sand and brush my hands. 'Let's keep going.'

The channel narrows and trees tower on either side. The beaches all but disappear. We penetrate deeper and deeper, and with every step I feel more alive. My senses hum.

'Jess.'

Frank's voice beside me is low and tense. I glance at him and follow his gaze. About one hundred metres upstream, a tree has collapsed from bank to bank, forming a bridge over the water. On it lies a jaguar.

Frank lifts the camera from his chest. But even with the zoom we are too far away. We walk, our paces measured to avoid splashing, our eyes never leaving the jaguar. Excitement wells in me. Nothing but air separates us from the big cat. Not the metal and glass of a car, nor the wooden hull of a boat. Here we are on an equal footing, as we were meant to be. My eyes burn and I blink. In that split second the jaguar is gone. There is no in-between, no slow slinking into the forest.

'Strange,' says Frank. 'I didn't think he'd be so scared of us.'

The sun is lower in the sky, the foliage now luminous, greens burnished with old-gold. Although it is tempting to explore further, we will find ourselves spending the night unprepared if we do not turn back soon.

'What do you think, just one more bend?' I ask. Frank agrees without hesitation.

As we round the meander, a beach, larger and higher than any we have seen so far, slopes gently up into the forest. Our shoes squelch as we step out of the current and walk onto the sand. Hollow, blackened tortoise shells litter the ground. There must be over fifty of them: pathetic, tiny domes, the size of cupped hands, scattered amongst great carapaces. Three stout baskets, woven from a single palm frond, lie abandoned next to the charred skull of a brocket deer and the voice box of a howler monkey. Frank and I stare at each other.

A pair of macaws flies overhead, their agonised cries startling me. We pick our way through the clutter. A dozen makeshift palm frond shelters dot the beach. At either end of every shelter are the ashes of a small fire over which the tortoises were roasted. Alive? I grimace. Between the hearths is space for two or perhaps three people to sleep.

Frank's soft 'Hey!' interrupts my thoughts. He motions me to the water's edge. At his feet is a set of human footprints, unexpectedly large, even allowing for time's erosion. We both know what we have stumbled upon. The hunting camp of a group

The author walking in the rainforest stream. (FH)

of so-called 'uncontacted' people, known by outsiders as the Mashco-Piro but who call themselves the Nomole, meaning 'brothers'. People who, due to past traumatic conflicts with what we call civilisation, choose to live in complete isolation from the rest of us, rejecting all we represent. People who walk naked, hunt with bows and arrows, use stone axes, and eat almost exclusively meat. I recall the jaguar's fear. It seems inconceivable that only a few hours' walk from here, engine-powered boats pass by daily, laden with tech-savvy tourists.

Logic tells us the Nomole are unlikely to be nearby —there is no acrid smell of smoke and the footprints are not fresh— but I cannot shake the feeling we are being watched. My skin prickles. We might have walked straight into them. What would have happened then? Would they have shied from us, run into the forest? Or would they have attacked us? With this comes the uneasy realisation we are intruders. The stream is not ours. It never was. We are trespassing.

I take a last look at the silent camp, suspended in a web of gathering shadows. Frank cannot resist taking some photographs, and even this benign act feels like an invasion.

We retrace our steps, subdued in thought, trying to reconcile what we have seen with our lives outside. We have not witnessed the past, nor the future, but a different present. The otter and jaguar, the Nomole, and ourselves: three separate, parallel worlds briefly intersecting, almost colliding, on the banks of a rainforest stream.

CHAPTER FOUR

A Giant at Risk

The Amazon forests and wetlands are no longer the uncharted wildernesses they were fifty, or even thirty, years ago. The nature conservation movement has realised the global importance of the region and bold steps have been taken to increase our knowledge of its biodiversity and to protect large portions for posterity. But the conservation movement is not alone; the footprint of the market economy and the realities of globalisation have become widely evident throughout, from the satellite dishes in native communities, to the gold mining tractors working day and night, to the abundance of imported Chinese clothes and plastic goods on the bustling streets of frontier towns. In a world hungry for raw materials eyes have turned to the Amazon.

A combination of physiological traits help to explain the generally low intrinsic rate of increase of giant otter populations and why even protected giant otter populations may take decades to recover from crashes like that induced by over-hunting. These include late age at first reproduction (giant otters attain

(JMR)

A world hungry for raw materials eyes have turned to the Amazon. (WW)

sexual maturity at roughly 2.5 years of age, but first breeding occurs on average two years later) and a long *generation time* – the time required for a generation of individuals to be born, reach sexual maturity, and reproduce – of approximately eight years. The degree of reproductive skew is high, meaning that only a third of the population consists of breeders, and small litters are produced only once a year. Moreover, a cub mortality of at least 30% and a further 50% mortality up to age of dispersal, not to mention high mortality amongst dispersers (especially males), slow their ability to colonise new areas. Extrinsic factors such as territory quality and distribution may also limit a population's rate of increase and its recovery. The vulnerability of giant otter populations to anthropogenic disturbance emphasises the importance of effective conservation measures, including protection of aquatic habitats in particular.

In order to enhance the range, nature, and efficiency of these conservation measures, the best possible use should be made of available research findings and conservation failures and successes. Before discussing specific conservation issues and solutions, however, we need to summarise past, current, and future threats faced by the giant otter. These can be divided into direct and indirect threats, with the former including hunting for the pelt trade, poaching, keeping giant otters as pets, and poorly managed tourism.

The giant otter is restricted to aquatic ecosystems in tropical forests and wetlands. Artisanal and large-scale mining, oil and gas production, road infrastructure, and hydroelectric projects are frequently undertaken in these same areas and usually pave the way for deforestation and timber extraction, commercial fisheries and aquaculture, and conversion of forests to cattle ranching and agriculture. Human settlements are growing rapidly, both due to immigration and high birth rates. Population growth leads to further intensification of human activities and hence increased degradation of aquatic as well as terrestrial habitats, thus indirectly affecting giant otter populations.

HUNTING, HUMAN/OTTER CONFLICT, AND OTTERS AS PETS

Hunting

Originally, the distribution range of the giant otter encompassed the entirety of lowland South America east of the Andes mountain chain, in Colombia, Venezuela, Ecuador, Peru, Bolivia, Guyana, Suriname, French Guiana, Paraguay, Uruguay, Argentina, and Brazil (Chile is the only country where the species has never occurred). But their dense and water-repellent fur, which equips them for a semi-aquatic existence, was highly prized by hunters, each luxurious pelt fetching the equivalent of US $50, equivalent to the wage for 10 days of backbreaking work on the land. By the time the pelt reached affluent North American, western European, and Japanese markets it was worth at least five and up to nine times as much as the hunter received.

Giant otters are highly susceptible to persecution: they are large, easily visible, group-living, and vocal. They are diurnal and occupy open habitats and stable territories. Their sign — latrines and dens — is easily recognisable and often visible, making it possible to identify areas of recent activity by a group. Individuals and groups usually react to people by approaching and periscoping noisily. Moreover, only the dominant pair produces young, only once a year. During the years of the pelt trade, these life history attributes of the species combined to make it extremely vulnerable.

According to a recent paper, an estimated 265,000 to 580,000 giant otters were killed in the Brazilian Amazon between 1904 and 1969, with a peak of maximum harvest in 1937. Between 1946 and 1973, almost 24,000 pelts were exported from Peru, while in Colombia 1,032 were exported in 1965, compared to 311 in 1970 and 85 in 1971 (these last figures reflect the dwindling numbers of otters in the wild). It has been estimated that Ecuador exported between 30,000 and 40,000 giant otter pelts in the period from 1940 to 1985. However, these statistics probably represent only a fraction of the true number killed

An old giant otter pelt clearly demonstrates the animal's impressive size. (FH)

Their habit of approaching potential threats make giant otters an easy target for hunters. (ND)

partly because the sale of many skins was not officially recorded due to smuggling or under invoicing by exporters, partly because carcasses sink if they are not soon recovered, and partly because dependent cubs are killed with the death of their parents.

By the late 1960s, exports were declining sharply as otters became scarcer. The unregulated demand was so great and populations were so thoroughly decimated that the oft-heard phrase 'driven to the brink of extinction' certainly applied to the giant otter. The river wolf eventually disappeared from much of its southern and easterly range including from Uruguay, Paraguay, and Argentina, and from the area east of the Tocantins and Parana basins in Brazil.

Commercial hunting was prohibited in many countries in the early 1970s and in 1973 the species was included under Appendix 1 of CITES (Convention of International Trade in Endangered Species). Venezuela was one of the last countries to ban hunting of giant otters in 1979. The international pelt market largely collapsed as a result, ending the economic benefits of hunting. Nonetheless, more than two decades after the ban, in 1998, giant otters were officially classified as Endangered (previously they were categorised as Vulnerable) in the IUCN Red List of Threatened Species. The giant otter has retained this status to the present day. In national Red Lists, the species

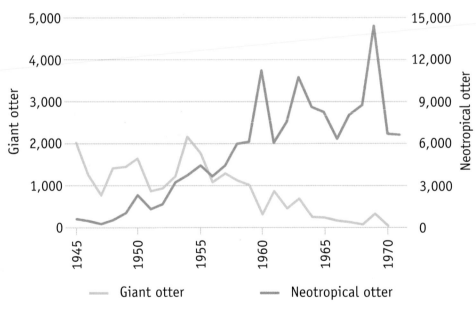

Exports of giant otter and Neotropical otter skins in Peru

Source: Brack-Egg, 1978

As giant otter pelt export decreased, probably reflecting a widespread population decline, that of Neotropical otter furs increased, indicating a switch from the larger and more easily hunted species to a less coveted option.

has been categorised as Critically Endangered in Ecuador, Paraguay, and Argentina; as Endangered in Peru, Colombia, Venezuela, French Guiana, and Bolivia; and as Vulnerable in Brazil. It is considered Extinct in Uruguay. The species is also protected by law in Suriname and Guyana, though this is rarely enforced.

HUMAN/OTTER CONFLICT

A market for giant otter fur no longer exists but this does not mean the giant otter is safe from poachers. Sporadic or opportunistic illegal hunting continues to this date and may have a disproportionate impact on small and hence fragile giant otter populations. More importantly, though the attitudes of people towards giant otters is often positive or neutral, in many parts of the giant otter's distribution range where the main economic activity is fishing, competition — real or perceived — between giant otters and commercial, subsistence, and sports fishermen, as well as loggers and miners wishing to supplement their diet with fish, is emerging as an increasingly important problem.

Conflict between giant otters and fishermen will be a recurring theme in the future. (Right, FH; below, WW)

Many riverine communities are heavily dependent on fish as their primary source of protein and/or income. Intensified fishing practices, in parallel with rapid human population growth as well as other factors such as alluvial gold mining and deforestation, have resulted in deterioration of fish stocks. This increases the possibility that local people use the giant otter as a scapegoat for dwindling fish resources, and that resentment against the species develops. In other parts, such as the Bolivian Amazon, fish resources are believed to be under-utilized and there is potential to increase fish production four-fold, once again possibly giving rise to increased conflict between people and giant otters in the long-term.

Fishermen often consider the species a nuisance and claim the otters inflict damage to expensive fishing nets and traps, or that their presence in fishing grounds causes disturbance. Otters have been accused of stealing bait from hooks, stored catches from inside canoes, and trapped fish from nets. It does not help that giant otters occasionally drown in nets, thus seemingly confirming culpability, or that they catch one fish after another with apparent ease and eat them in full view above water. Moreover, giant otter latrines, covered in fish remains, are often confused with places where the animals eat rather than defecate, thus reinforcing the impression that giant otters consume huge quantities of fish. The situation is further exacerbated by the belief that giant otters are recovering more rapidly or are more numerous, and groups larger, than is often the case.

In north-eastern Peru, giant otters were blamed for declining stocks of arowana (*Osteoglossum bicirrhosum*), the juveniles of which are sold in their millions to the aquarium trade. A perceived increase in giant otter populations coincided with a fall in the numbers of arowana harvested by some households, although there was no evidence to support the relationship. Arowana are slow to mature and fecundity is relatively low, rendering the species vulnerable to overexploitation. Fish-farming is also increasing rapidly within the giant otter's range and may prove to be a source of conflict and habitat degradation in the future.

Resentment arising from perceived competition and material and/or financial loss in some areas is such that local communities have reached the point of formally requesting intervention, in the form of culls, from local authorities. Or they have taken steps in their own hands. A total of 21 giant otters were reportedly killed over an undefined period between 2006 and 2009 in the Uacari Sustainable Development Reserve, in the state of Amazonas, Brazil. In 2011–2012, the Kanamari indigenous people promoted a giant otter killing spree in their territory (Território Indígena Kanamari, adjacent to the SDR Uacari, Brazil), based on their perception that the species was overhunting the river turtle population. The community leader bought 300 cartridges and distributed these amongst other hunters; 64 giant otters were reportedly shot. Such incidents of targeted killing increase the extinction risk of small sub-populations in a watershed.

Although giant otters do consume large numbers of fish (up to four kilograms per adult otter per day), several studies into the troubled relationship between giant otters and fishermen indicate that direct competition is not significant since the degrees of overlap in human and otter diets, and between fish species consumed by giant otters and those exploited by commercial fisheries, are small. It is, then, not so much an increase in giant otter numbers (in some areas) or their appetite for fish that is the main cause of reduced catches, but overexploitation of stocks by fishermen themselves and a lack of adequate management of these fisheries, many of which employ unsustainable equipment such as monofilament nets or methods such as poisoning using agrochemicals. There is thus a problem of interests, where fishermen are unwilling to accept they may themselves be the cause of fish stock declines and look elsewhere for an explanation. Conflict is greater near large human settlements in aquatic systems with low fish productivity, while hostility towards giant otters is reduced in communities with traditional fishing practices for subsistence.

Some villagers display the giant otter's skin as adornments in their homes, or use otters for target practice and entertainment, or kill them out of ignorance and fear caused by their large size, 'aggressive' behaviour, and prominent canines. In November 1978, a man died as a result of bites inflicted by giant otters when he rescued a boy who had fallen into their enclosure at the Brasilia Zoo. This incident apparently generated considerable and long-lasting antipathy towards giant otters in Brazil.

KEEPING OTTERS AS PETS

It is not uncommon for giant otter cubs to be captured in the belief that they would make cute pets, or for financial gain. Offences are often unwitting, due to ignorance of the law, of conservation practice, and of the basic needs of the species. Though occurring on an as yet minor scale, this habit is pernicious throughout the species' distribution range. Cubs are relatively easily caught or taken from dens when very young and in some cases the parents are killed to procure them. Many youngsters die within a few days or weeks from malnutrition or poor husbandry conditions, or are killed in accidents. If they do survive, their ravenous appetite for fish soon gets them into trouble: feeding an extra mouth over and above a villager's own needs and that of his family is a daunting task. As cubs grow they often become unmanageable. Some animals are confiscated by authorities and handed over to local zoos that are not always adequately equipped or staffed to deal with them. Rehabilitation is a difficult and lengthy process and frequently ends in failure, even when undertaken by experts. The taking of cubs is highly disruptive to giant otter families, occasionally resulting in the complete disintegration of a group. After a hunter snatched a pair of cubs from their parents in her study area in Suriname, Duplaix found that the adults lost their territory to a neighbouring family group. A few weeks later, the female and a sub adult disappeared, leaving her mate on his own.

A Neotropical otter cub is offered for sale. Otter cubs are all too easily dug out of the den or captured while their family is away. Trafficking of young animals is a problem throughout the Amazon. (FT)

Cubs may be confiscated and offered to local zoos that are often ill equipped, like this one in Iquitos, northern Peru. (FH)

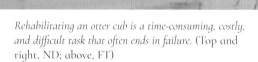

Rehabilitating an otter cub is a time-consuming, costly, and difficult task that often ends in failure. (Top and right, ND; above, FT)

Giant otter cubs belong in the wild, with their families. (JMR)

NATURE TOURISM: FRIEND OR FOE?

Nature tourism, often referred to as ecotourism, also presents challenges. It is a rapidly growing industry worldwide and is usually regarded as ecologically sustainable. It is also the only large-scale economic activity permitted in protected areas, many of which harbour remnant giant otter populations and play a key role in conservation of the species. Nature tourism thus has considerable potential to support wildlife conservation and bring much-needed revenues, and there is increasing interest in giant otters as a key tourism attraction in many parts of its range, only surpassed in popularity by the jaguar.

It is not easy to watch large mammals in South American rainforests; they are few and far between and many inhabit the forest canopy or are active mainly at night. In contrast, the giant otter is one of very few large, endangered mammals that are relatively easily observed. Rainforest tourism concentrates along rivers and lakes, almost completely overlapping giant otter habitat. The species occupies stable territories that often become accessible, reliable destinations for tourist excursions. Giant otters are highly social, living in vocal family groups that hunt by day. They are attractive and active; in short, this charismatic animal easily becomes a rewarding focal point for tourism. But to place too much emphasis on a single species as a tourist attraction is risky: it can result in disappointed visitors if their expectations are not met, in guides who feel pressured to procure photographic opportunities and so may go to unacceptable lengths to satisfy their customers, and in otters that learn, through bitter experience, to avoid human presence.

Often, it is a question of misunderstanding. Giant otters react to people as they do to caimans, perceiving us as a potential threat. The otters approach and circle the boat to within a few metres, periscoping and uttering warning snorts. This behaviour is identical to that displayed by otters when confronting a caiman, who generally respond by retreating to the shore or to deeper water. Sometimes a full blown confrontation results. When the caiman retreats the otters usually follow it a short distance before returning to their original activity. However, interactions with boats normally take a different course. The attitude of the otters is often misinterpreted as tameness. Humans then attempt to get even closer to them, out of curiosity or to take a better photograph, so that they eventually feel forced to move on. In future encounters, the otters will learn to steer clear of this 'super predator', and tourists will no longer have satisfactory viewing experiences.

Tourists may also approach otter dens unintentionally as they move along shorelines to observe monkeys or birds. Boat traffic can have a serious impact on giant otter presence, depending on the intensity and speed of traffic, and the size of the boats. And not only do we interfere with their activities on the water, we also build infrastructure and clear paths directly along shorelines, thereby preventing otters from constructing their dens or latrines.

A serious consequence of tourism is lowered reproductive success. The height of the tourism season in Peru is preceded by a peak in giant otter births; by August, most otter families are rearing vulnerable cubs. Giant otters, especially the parents, are much more nervous at this time of year. In zoos, it was discovered that females may fail to nurse, and even eat, their cubs as a result of stress induced by visitors. Though they are surrounded by people all year round, when they have cubs, captive otters become highly sensitive to outside disturbance. This behaviour is mirrored in the wild. We have observed families remove their cubs in haste when fishermen or tourists came too close to a den, and each den change carries a risk of predation or getting lost for the cubs.

Between 1990 and 1996/1997 the otter group on Cocha Salvador exhibited low reproductive success, producing only one litter of two cubs in six years. This litter was born in the rainy season which is unusual in Manu; the majority of cubs are born during the dry season which coincides with a peak in tourist numbers. In 1998, a new otter group occupied the lake, producing 13 cubs in five years. It is thought that the low reproductive success of the first otter family may be attributed to poorly managed tourism between 1991 and 1996; several tourist groups were observed chasing the otters and approaching the den to check if they were inside.

MINING, WATER POLLUTION, AND FOSSIL FUELS

Mining

Gold mining, legal and illegal, artisanal as well as industrial, is the most widespread mining activity in the giant otter's range, with iron ore and bauxite mining also of importance. The Guiana Shield region (encompassing Suriname, Guyana, French Guiana, Venezuela, and northern Brazil) and south-eastern Peru are particularly affected by the main impacts of artisanal and small-scale gold mining. Gold occurs as dust in thin layers of sediments, between the surface and a depth of several metres, of many rivers and their floodplains. The gold is alluvial in origin, having been transported from primary deposits in the Andes to floodplain areas over millions of years. This is why gold is found not only in current river channels and floodplains but over a much wider region including old floodplains.

Mining methods have changed from small-scale manual panning in the past, to more sophisticated and environmentally damaging operations today. Land in floodplains is cleared of forest and blasted with high pressure water hoses. The resulting large quantities of soil and sediments, which tend to be naturally rich in mercury, are then filtered through a sluice and elemental mercury, a highly poisonous metal, is added. The mercury forms a strong bond with gold and separates it from the river sediments. The amalgam is then heated, in the field or in gold shops in nearby towns, to separate the metals. Artisanal and small-scale gold mining have surpassed fossil fuel combustion as the largest anthropogenic source of mercury to

A range of artisanal gold mining operations in south-eastern Peru, from a simple wheelbarrow-and-hose arrangement, to barges, and shoreline camps. (FH)

Gold mining barges form rafts at particularly rich or promising locations. (WW)

Mercury (left, FH) is used in the sluices of mining barges where it binds to fine gold particles to produce a gold-mercury amalgam (centre, WW) which, upon burning with a blow torch, reveals the precious metal (right, WW).

the global atmosphere. One to four grams of mercury are necessary to produce one gram of gold; between 20 to 40% of the mercury used is released directly into aquatic ecosystems while another 20 to 40% is lost to the atmosphere. The release of large quantities of mercury directly into the environment is thus considered a significant threat, with migration of contaminated fish and long-range atmospheric transport of mercury probably increasing the miner's area of influence.

There is an ongoing debate on the fate of mercury in areas affected by gold mining as well as the many interrelated factors that influence it, and the findings of numerous studies are sometimes contradictory. What is known is that mercury may cause multiple symptomatic effects, such as neurochemical, reproductive, behavioural, physiological, immunological, and histological changes, affecting the health and survival of species that are exposed. Concentrations of over 1.9 milligrams of mercury per kilogram of muscle is lethal to fish and 0.5 milligrams per kilogram is harmful, affecting reproduction by reducing egg production, viability of sperm, frequency of hatching, and survival of offspring. Furthermore, environmental factors in the Amazon, including high temperatures and high bacterial activity, slightly acidic conditions, and low oxygen levels, favour methylation (the transformation of inorganic to the organic mercury compound, methylmercury, which is highly neurotoxic) and hence absorption into body tissues.

Mercury is known to bioaccumulate and biomagnify – increase in concentration going through successive levels of the aquatic food chain – resulting in potentially toxic levels in top predator and migratory fish as well as omnivores and other piscivores, such as giant otters. Mercury poisoning in fish-eating wild mink and otters has been reported in North America and Europe, with changes in the brain occurring at dietary methylmercury concentrations of 0.5 milligrams per kilogram. Several studies have determined that mercury concentrations in fish in or downstream from mining areas are sufficiently high to cause toxification in animals at higher trophic levels in the Amazon. A study in French Guiana demonstrated marked biomagnification of mercury in the food chain, with muscle tissue from a piscivorous species containing 715 times the mercury level found in a herbivorous species. The probability of catching a *Hoplias aimara* of one kilogram or more and exceeding the World Health Organization safety limit of 2.5 milligrams per kilogram was 91%.

Similarly, a Manu study analysing mercury and methyl mercury levels in fish muscles and giant otter scats found that total mercury levels in 68% of fish muscle samples exceeded the maximum tolerable level for the Eurasian otter (*Lutra lutra*) and 17.6% exceeded 0.5 milligrams per kilogram of fresh weight, the most common standard for human consumption. However, little or no mercury was detected in otter scats. In the Pantanal, a study found that 89% of samples obtained from liver and muscle tissues of fish caught on the rivers Bento Gomes and Cuiaba (in Mato Grosso) and Paraguai (in Mato Grosso do Sul) showed detectable levels of mercury. Of those, 27% contained mercury levels above the maximum concentration allowed for human consumption. However, the necropsy of two giant otters found floating in the Rio Negro in the Pantanal revealed mercury concentrations in hair, liver, kidney and muscle tissues that appeared to be at levels below those associated with toxicity. While there is no evidence as yet that mercury contamination of fish is affecting the health and survival of giant otters, there are clearly grounds for concern.

Peru is the fifth largest gold producer in the world and the Department of Madre de Dios generates 70% of Peru's artisanal gold production. Helped by new roads, the extent of gold mining in the Madre de Dios region increased in tandem with the soaring price of gold – reaching a record high of almost US$1,890 per ounce in 2011 (though it has since fallen somewhat, at time of writing it looks set to increase again) – from less than 10,000 hectares in 1999 to more than 50,000 hectares in 2012, which exceeds loss from ranching, agriculture, and logging combined. Peru's mercury imports have increased exponentially (about 175 tonnes in 2009), 95% of which is used in artisanal gold mining. It has been estimated that between 10,000 and 30,000 miners are active, making up nearly 50% of the local economy. The watersheds of several rivers are now reminiscent of lunar landscapes and are probably the largest, continuous devastated mining landscapes in the Amazon Basin.

Before and after: While international gold prices remain high, gold mining is the most economically productive activity on a per hectare basis. But what about the not-so-hidden costs? (WW)

A study on the Madre de Dios River demonstrated a gradient of increasing mercury contamination and food web accumulation in the river downstream of mining areas. It found that mercury concentrations in sediment, suspended solids, and fish muscle tissue in areas downstream of gold mining were higher relative to locations upstream of mining. Fish tissue mercury concentrations were observed at levels representing a public health threat, with more than one-third of carnivorous fish exceeding the international health standard of 0.5 milligrams per kilogram.

Dredging for gold also results in large amounts of suspended particulate matter in water courses, affecting productivity by reducing light penetration, smothering bottom-dwelling algae species and benthic invertebrates, and affecting fish respiratory systems. In French Guiana, where the areas impacted by gold mining increased from 210 to 11,470 hectares (a 50-fold increase over six years), increased turbidity resulting from gold mining did not significantly affect fish biomass and species richness,

Many large catfish caught in or downstream from gold mining areas are contaminated with mercury, sometimes to levels not deemed suitable for human consumption. (WW)

but fish taxonomic composition was strongly influenced and the structure of fish communities was significantly affected, with smaller, opportunistic fishes favoured at the expense of larger, habitat-specialist species. In 2006, French laws prohibited the use of mercury for gold mining in French Guiana. However, this has had negligible impact on gold mining activities in the country, with mercury now entering illegally from Brazil or Suriname.

A key issue is that the environmental problems generated greatly hinder the development of sustainable forestry, fisheries, or tourism activities in these areas, perpetuating mining as the only economic alternative. And since it may take many years, or even decades, for a water body to recover from gold mining disturbance, depending on its duration and severity, there are fears that the long-term risk associated with gold mining may only become apparent in the future and that mercury contamination and its effects will persist for several decades even if effective control of mercury input is achieved.

Water pollution

Toxic chemical disasters and pollution are a growing danger to the quality of aquatic habitats and fish stocks in many areas of tropical South America. They result not only in the release of huge quantities of harmful chemicals and heavy metals, but also lead to direct and indirect large-scale habitat destruction. In 2015, the biggest environmental disaster in Brazil's history saw 32 to 40 million cubic metres of mining waste destroy a river system in Minas Gerais after a tailings dam collapsed. Another method for gold production is leaching with cyanide, also a highly toxic compound. In August 1995, 400 million gallons of cyanide-laced slurry drained into the Essequibo River in Guyana after the Omai tailings dam breached. Large numbers of dead fish and a thick slick of waste on the rivers caused the Guyana government to prohibit the use of water for drinking and household use immediately after the spill. The inadequacy of legal and regulatory frameworks is a major factor that leads to weak or non-existing monitoring of the environmental standards of small and large mining companies.

Fossil fuels

Oil and gas exploration and production is widespread in tropical South America, with Venezuela, Colombia, Ecuador, Peru, and Bolivia being important centres of activity. About 180 oil and gas blocks cover approximately 690,000 square kilometres of the exceptionally species-rich western Amazon. In Ecuador and Peru, oil and gas blocks cover more than two-thirds of the Amazon. Since the 1970s, numerous large projects have been established, including several in the central Ecuadorian Amazon, the Urucu gas project in Brazil, and the Camisea gas project in Peru.

Although in recent years there have been improvements in drilling and oil production technology and practices, experience in the Amazon region shows nonetheless that hydrocarbon extraction leads to multiple serious threats to biodiversity and protected areas. Accidental or deliberate spills of oil, effluents, and drilling muds have had a particularly harmful impact on water bodies. In most operations, environmental and production standards are still very low, with hundreds of environmental disasters to prove this. Over a period of two decades, Texaco (now owned by Chevron) severely and extensively contaminated Ecuadorian rainforests, releasing over 16 million gallons of oil into aquatic systems from ruptures in its main pipelines. Further damage was caused by more than 4.3 million gallons of untreated waste that was discharged into the watershed daily. The much newer Camisea pipeline, in south-eastern Peru, ruptured five times, causing major spills, within the first 18 months of operation. Elsewhere, headlines such as 2016's '$1bn to clean up the oil in Peru's northern Amazon' feature regularly in the news.

Another direct impact includes deforestation for access roads, drilling platforms, and pipelines. But direct impacts from oil and gas production are not always the most serious; indirect effects can be far more insidious, arising from easy access to previously remote primary forest provided by new oil roads and pipeline routes, causing increased habitat fragmentation, illegal logging, unsustainable hunting, and deforestation arising from human settlement. Impacts along new access roads cannot be adequately controlled or managed and a major road-less oil project in Ecuador's

Lakes and rivers are the highways of much of the Amazon. Giant otters avoid areas of heavy boat traffic but the alternative... (JG)

... is more destructive still. Where roads penetrate forest, human settlement and consumption of local resources invariably follow. (WW)

Block 10 was the region's first example of a more sensitive development model. More innovative still was the offer of Ecuador's President, Rafael Correa, to leave the untapped oil fields beneath the most remote and intact parts of Yasuní National Park, the country's principal Amazonian protected area, permanently underground in exchange for compensation from the international community. However, six years later, in 2013, this groundbreaking initiative was abandoned, with lack of concrete international commitment cited as the main reason.

DEFORESTATION, INTENSIVE AGRICULTURE, AND HUMAN COLONISATION (HABITAT DESTRUCTION)

International and national demands for tropical timber, soybeans, free-range beef, and livestock feed has led to extensive deforestation in the Amazon. Amazonia lies inside nine nations, but 80% of deforestation has been in Brazil, with 70% of that caused by cattle ranching. There is also an accelerating demand for bio fuels and palm oil. The rapid increase in human population in lowland South America has further contributed to the felling of tropical rainforest. The human population of the Brazilian Amazon, for example, increased from six million in 1960 to 25 million in 2010 and the forest cover for this region has declined to about 80% of its original area. Deforestation results in increased erosion and associated water quality degradation which in turn impact fish stocks. Most human settlement is concentrated along or near water bodies; rivers

The forests of the Amazon are feeling the heat of a world economy hungry for resources. (ABT)

Reduced to a number, mahogany trees await their turn at a sawmill. (WW)

A portable saw mill at work near an illegal logging camp. (FH)

Timber on its way to American and European markets. (FH)

represent major navigation and transport routes and giant otters are now entirely absent in most areas of heavy motorised river traffic. The construction of roads by oil, mining, and logging companies, as well as government projects such as dams, has led to human encroachment even in the remote interiors of many countries.

The large-scale conversion of primary forests into monoculture crops and forest plantations may cause disruption of flow patterns of water courses and of shorelines in use by giant otters. Many riverine habitats undergo annual burns to create and improve pasture for cattle. In the Pantanal, a giant otter den was struck by fire, which resulted in its abandonment. The nutrient-poor soil of the Amazon basin supports crops and pasture for only a few years: this promotes further clearing and burning of forest. Water pollution by agricultural pesticides and herbicides is also

The demand for beef is one of the leading drivers of rainforest destruction. (WW)

regarded as a threat to the species. Wetlands like the Pantanal are susceptible to this type of contamination, constantly draining and concentrating runoff chemicals from surrounding plateaus where extensive agriculture dominates.

Habitat destruction may exacerbate the geographical isolation of remnant giant otter populations, through a process known as fragmentation, thereby reducing genetic fitness. Hence, the future for giant otter populations inhabiting areas which are not protected and monitored is bleak. However, protected areas alone will not guarantee the long-term survival of the species; the concept of hydrological management (including zoning and the creation of corridors) and planning should be put into practice, as will be discussed further in Chapter Five.

Dams

The construction of dams and creation of artificial lakes to meet rising energy demands and for supplying water for domestic, agricultural, and industrial purposes form an important part of the economic development of the Neotropics. A study of hydropower projects in Ecuador, Peru, and Bolivia documented 142 dams that already exist or are under construction, and a further 160, most classified as high- or medium-impact, that are proposed for rivers draining the Andean foothills. Two other mega dams were completed in 2012 on the Madeira River in Brazil. Although many Andean dams may be far from Amazonian lowlands inhabited by giant otters, their profound alteration of sediment and flow regimes is likely to transform natural systems downstream. For example, existing (mostly small) dams have already fragmented the tributary networks of six of eight major Andean Amazon river basins, though the main stems of rivers remain intact. If the proposed dams are constructed, losses in river network connectivity could increase by between 35% and 50%, making significant main-stem fragmentation for five of eight major Andean Amazon rivers a real possibility.

Dams drastically alter river channel and floodplain geomorphology for thousands of kilometres downstream by controlling sediment deposition, river meandering, and oxbow lake formation. Highland rivers contribute 93% of sediments to the Amazon River, and roughly half of its flow, as well as vast quantities of organic matter and nutrients. Dams also influence the hydrological regimes of rivers downstream (leading to fluctuations in flow and changes in water temperature that occur out of sync with seasonal patterns), as well as habitat suitability and resource availability, with resulting impacts on fish populations. Many economically and ecologically important Amazonian fish spawn only in Andean-fed rivers, including long-distance migrant species of large catfish and Characins favoured by giant otters, such as *Prochilodus nigricans*. Furthermore, new or cheaper electricity could further stimulate road construction, mining, or deforestation, thus compounding the problem. There is evidence to suggest that dams located downstream of gold mining areas may enhance methylation of inorganic mercury in the deep anoxic parts of their reservoirs, resulting in mercury concentrations many times higher than those upstream.

Giant otters are able to use reservoirs of hydroelectric dams year-round, including for breeding, provided the species previously occurred in the area. Factors related to the degree of human presence and use after damming, the baseline features of pre-filling habitats, as well as the physical and chemical properties of floodwaters, overall landscape topography, and the type of dam constructed, will influence quality outcomes for the river wolf.

A long-term giant otter study has been underway since 2001 following the filling of the Balbina Reservoir, in Brazil. The Balbina dam, built in 1987, flooded almost 444,000 hectares of primary forest, created over 3,500 islands, and increased the open-water surface area and total perimeter available to otters by a factor of 63 and 9 respectively. Some 25 years after damming, however, the estimated giant otter population size was only twice greater than that estimated before filling, and 4.5 times smaller than predicted given the total habitat area available. Low habitat quality in terms of low fish productivity and scarcity of suitable sites for denning and territory demarcation are cited as the cause. So far, no population has been monitored both prior to and post reservoir construction/filling in order to evaluate the real impact of dams.

Other massive projects such as the Initiative for Integration of the Regional Infrastructure of South America (IIRSA), which is destined to link South American economies to global markets through a portfolio of large-scale transport, energy infrastructure, and telecommunication networks, particularly in remote and isolated regions, is likely to have profound and far-reaching consequences for freshwater ecosystems as a whole, and thus for the giant otter.

DOMESTIC ANIMAL DISEASES

Diseases of domestic animals which spread to wild populations may cause serious mortality. In Tanzania in 1994, canine distemper virus caused the death of a third of Serengeti National Park's lion population and is believed to have been transmitted to wildlife by infected domestic dogs owned by local tribesmen. In South America, settlers and natives often keep dogs, even in protected areas. Contact with faeces from an infected dog could well expose giant otters to canine distemper virus and canine parvovirus, both known to have been fatal to young giant otters in captivity. In August 1995, Schenck collected blood samples from dogs in and around Manu to investigate the potential of this threat. The results indicated that the local population of dogs carried antibodies to both diseases and that the latter therefore had occurred recently in the area. Infection could occur also in remote areas since dispersing transient otters and people hunting with dogs travel large distances, with potential for contact and infection of immunologically naïve populations.

Giant otters seem to fear this pig of the forest, the white-lipped peccary (Tayassu pecari). In the 1980s, the species suffered an abrupt, region-wide decline thought to be caused by an epidemic disease transmitted from livestock. (Left, JG; bottom, FH)

CLIMATE CHANGE

Though the effects of climate change have only recently begun to be studied in parts of the Amazon, modelling of future scenarios provide some idea of the magnitude of impacts at regional as well as global scales. Over the next decades, climate change is expected to influence water temperatures, rainfall, hydrological regimes, seasonality, patterns of flooding, and levels of dissolved oxygen. These will likely affect migration patterns and distribution limits of fish which in turn will impact the distribution of dependent species, including the giant otter, possibly resulting in contraction of its range through habitat loss.

In recent decades the rate of warming in Amazonia has been about 0.25°C per decade. There has also been a drying trend in northern Amazonia since the mid-1970s and extreme events such as droughts and fires are already being felt in the Brazilian Amazon. Changes in rainfall, particularly during the dry season, are probably the most critical factor determining the climatic fate of the Amazon, and the region's forests have a substantial influence on regional and continental climates. Hence, their removal can itself be a driver of global climate change.

Rainforests may become seasonally flammable in dry years, yet fire is a rare occurrence and so many tree species lack adaptations that allow them to survive even low-intensity fires. Fire use for land management is widespread in rural Amazonia. Logging and forest fragmentation also increase the flammability of forests by

Climate change is likely to have far-reaching consequences for the survival of a multitude of Amazon species, including the giant otter. (ABT)

For how much longer will the Amazon wilderness belong to the giant otter? (JMR)

providing combustion material, allowing sunlight to penetrate the forest interior, and drying out the understory and leaf litter thereby further increasing the fuel load on the forest floor. This synergism between fragmentation and fire is becoming increasingly important. Once burnt, a forest becomes more vulnerable to recurrent burns, drought further increases fire susceptibility, and multiple fires slow forest re-growth and release smoke into the atmosphere, thus reducing rainfall. During the severe 2005 drought in south-western Amazonia, when dry season temperatures were 3 to 5°C warmer than normal and rainfall was only 33% to 65% of average values, there was substantial penetration of fires from agricultural areas into the surrounding, temporarily flammable forests, as well as a decline in growth and a significant increase in tree mortality. A similarly severe but more extensive drought occurred in 2010, affecting more than half of the basin and resulting in a record low river discharge at Manaus.

In summary, then, it seems likely that mining activities, infrastructure development, and the widespread conversion of forest into agricultural and pasture lands will continue unabated in the near future as part of the economic development of Amazonian countries. Brazil, which represents roughly three quarters of the giant otter's current distribution range, is especially important, with its Amazon region experiencing the highest human population growth of the whole country. Despite the concerted efforts of authorities, civil society, and numerous scientists, we can expect expansion into and colonisation of new regions and continued intensive exploitation of natural resources, resulting in the destruction of forests, reduction of water quality, and overfishing.

A Piece of Cake

'It's uta,' Frank said. He slumped into a chair and sighed.

Such an innocent, little word. Yet one every researcher who sets foot in the Peruvian rainforest dreads to hear. We looked with dismay at the ulcer on his wrist. It had refused to heal despite weeks of cleansing and sticking on fresh plasters. It was actually getting *deeper* day by day, and this had finally prompted Frank to go to the doctor. Now he was back with the verdict.

Uta, or *leishmaniasis*, is caused by a protozoan transmitted by forest-dwelling sand flies. While not fatal, if left untreated, a second form of the tropical disease can develop in as many as eighty percent of cases, attacking the mucus membranes around the mouth and nose. The doctor, warming to his task, had shared graphic photographs of the leprous disfigurement that may follow, and Frank had at once headed for the nearest pharmacist.

'I have to have a course of daily injections. Thirty of them. Some kind of antimony compound. Apparently it's like a form of chemotherapy.'

'Yikes. What about side effects?' I asked.

'Well, the doctor said I'll feel tired and achy and I might lose my appetite.' Frank grimaced. 'Also, I can't drink any alcohol for six months.'

'Great. That's an end to our Manu field trip then. We can't go if you need to have an injection every day.'

'Yeah, that had occurred to me too. But we can't delay our departure. Soon the rains will start.' Frank shrugged and picked at something on his jeans. 'So I've got an idea.'

I narrowed my eyes at him. 'You're not thinking what I'm thinking.'

He was. 'You're a biologist. It's no big deal. Biologists do it all the time. What do you say?'

I considered 'it'. I had never administered an injection before. But the more I thought about it, the more the idea appealed to me. This was my chance to be a true, hard-bitten field researcher, like the ones you see in TV documentaries. I wasn't going to tranquillise a cheetah for radio collaring or dart a charging elephant — nothing as glamorous as that. But even the prospect of injecting my hubby every day seemed exciting.

'Okay, you're on. I'll be nurse.' Then I remembered something. Frank once fainted while watching me being immunised against rabies. 'Hang on. What about--'

'Good, that's decided then.' Frank rose briskly and headed to the kitchen. 'Time for a beer. It'll be my last for a while.'

Though I privately considered it unnecessary, Frank persuaded me to ask a professional nurse for a demonstration on getting the fifteen millilitres of fluid into his bloodstream. I observed her competent movements closely; she made it look easy. The following morning, Day Two of the treatment, Frank submitted to his jab from me, under the nurse's supervision. I was right. It *was* easy.

'A piece of cake, nothing to it,' I said. We departed for Manu later that day, a small cardboard box of twenty-eight antimony vials tucked in my rucksack, feeling pleased we were dealing responsibly with the situation.

Even now I find it painful to think of Day Three. The mood was light hearted as we began, gradually becoming philosophical — 'Obviously yesterday was a fluke, you can't expect to get it right first time, every time' — but by my fourth attempt, the strain was apparent on Frank's averted face. He suffered seven punctures before I succeeded with the eighth. There wasn't much left in the syringe by then, most of the liquid having formed telltale knots under his skin. Frank gave me a hug and told me this failure was just a one-off. I smiled weakly. That night I lay awake in our tent for hours, brooding about the days ahead.

Dawn in the rainforest is a symphony of pearlescent shades, tendrils of mist rising over the river, and the drowsy calls of stirring wildlife. But I was far from tranquil the next morning as I gathered the items I would need: the tourniquet, syringe, needle, disinfectant swab, and glass vial of antimony. Frank prepared breakfast and teased our two Peruvian field assistants, Zacarias and Wilfredo. He seemed relaxed, but I wasn't fooled.

The author treating her husband for leishmaniasis.

'Dawn in the rainforest is a symphony of pearlescent shades.' (FH)

When we had eaten, he sat opposite me and held out his arm. I circled his biceps with the length of elastic rubber and watched the vein at the inside of his elbow bulge. At least he had obliging blood vessels.

Right, I thought, as I cleaned the site thoroughly. *Take it one step at a time.*

First I had to break off the top of the glass vial with a smart snap. I glanced at Frank's face. He gazed at the river, feigning unconcern. My confidence wavered.

Come on, Jess, you can do this.

Holding the vial firmly, I applied pressure. Instead of breaking off cleanly, its neck crumbled between my fingers.

Oh, wonderful.

Extracting a new vial from the box was not an option; we couldn't replace it out there in the bush and the thirty shots had to be delivered without missing a day if the treatment was to succeed.

Don't panic. Remember, keep everything sterile.

I pushed the needle out of its packaging and onto the syringe. Next I dipped the needle into the liquid, careful to keep the tip away from any glass splinters lurking at the bottom.

Now, just pull back the plunger and suck it up.

I flicked my finger against the syringe to get rid of a few air bubbles. Holding the needle against Frank's skin, I drew a breath. Gently, I inserted the tip and pulled back the plunger. A wisp of blood billowed in the liquid. I exhaled.

You're in the vein. So far, so good. Now inject. Slowly…

In that moment, my world became the needle. I was that needle.

Please… please, please…

A lump began to bulge. The fluid was not entering the vein but accumulating under the skin.

WHY? What am I doing wrong?

I clenched my teeth. Frank's eyes refused to meet mine. When I bungled my fifth effort, my resolve faltered. I was going to kill Frank, not cure him. Zacarias and Wilfredo hovered in the background, watching us covertly with doubtful expressions. Later, they took Frank aside. Didn't he know the surest way to recover from uta was to stop sharing a tent with me? They also counselled treating the wound with local remedies such as banana skin pulp or battery acid to quicken the healing process. Battery acid — heck, why hadn't I thought of that? Running the ulcer under a belt sander would probably help too.

Matters did not improve over the next few days, and I seriously considered returning to civilisation where I could release myself from this burden. Frank's bruised arms looked like he had been mainlining for weeks.

One afternoon we met a tourist who happened to mention he worked in a hospital. I confessed my problems to Ian; he told me it was simply a question of mastering the knack. I nodded politely, while mentally rolling my eyes.

The following morning, I showed Ian my technique. Having my every move scrutinised by a pro was nerve-wracking and my fingers trembled as I prepared to penetrate Frank's vein. Ian leaned forward, eyes intent. I inserted the needle and pulled back the plunger of the syringe, hoping for the plume of blood. There it was.

'Good. Now, here's the trick. Push the tip of the needle a little deeper into the vein and then follow along it a few millimetres before depressing the plunger,' Ian said. 'Wait. Hold the syringe at less of an angle.'

I steadied my hand and imagined the vein running under and parallel to the skin. Then I did as I was told. No treacherous knot appeared. The last of the fluid flowed smoothly into Frank's bloodstream. 'Yes!' I yelped. 'Oh, yes!'

Ian beamed at me. 'Now you should be able to manage fine on your own.'

The next day, I succeeded in my first attempt. Unaided. The elation I felt must be like scoring a goal for one's country in the final of the World Cup.

Over the following weeks I delivered his shots with a blasé panache even a seasoned nurse would have envied. Until the awful moment arrived when, back home, my mother-in-law decided she wanted to see me in action…

CHAPTER FIVE

Saving the Giant Otter

WHY PROTECT THE GIANT OTTER?

According to the IUCN Red list assessment for the species, published in 2015, the giant otter is categorised as Endangered because experts have good reason to expect a potential reduction of 50% in giant otter population size within a 25 year-period. Let that sink in for a moment: we stand to lose half of the world's giant otters within just a quarter of a century, or one human generation. Clearly, something needs to be done to avoid re-visiting the severe population decline experienced by the species during the pelt trade decades.

There are both ethical and economic reasons for supporting giant otter conservation. On the ethical front, human thought is slowly moving away from an anthropocentric view of the world, a view in which only human beings are worthy of ethical consideration and where other living creatures are seen only as means to human ends. We are beginning to realise that other species also have intrinsic value, that rights are not the exclusive domain of mankind, and that we must be responsible stewards of nature's diversity.

(FH)

Science is also doing its bit. Traits such as culture and self awareness, once seen as uniquely human, are being shown to exist in multiple species thanks to recent research efforts around the globe. Many species have collections of unique behavioural traits that exist in one population but not in another or in one group of a population but not in the rest. These traits are not inherited, but are taught by parents to offspring, and passed down from generation to generation. This has been documented not only in cetaceans and the great apes, mammals from which we have learnt to expect a degree of intelligence and sophistication, but also in birds and fish.

It is said that the hallmark of civilised nations is that they treat their more vulnerable members — their children, their handicapped, their elderly — with respect and consideration. In line with this idea, many groups of people around the world are making a more concerted effort to extend this respect and dignity to other non-human animals and even to entire rivers. Several studies regarding our relationships with domestic animals have also confirmed that people who treat animals with cruelty are more likely to treat fellow humans in the same manner; violence directed at animals is often a precursor of violence directed at people. Thus, when we learn to respect and conserve wildlife and wild places, we will have taken a firm step towards the creation of a more respectful, peaceful, and equitable society for ourselves.

In economic terms, probably one of the strongest justifications for protecting the giant otter is the rapidly growing nature tourism or ecotourism sector. Tourism as a whole in Peru, for example, has grown from 1.4 million international tourists in 2004 to 3.6 million in 2017, an annual increase of 17%. In contrast, tourism to Peru's protected natural areas is growing at an annual rate of over 30%, with 1.8 million tourists (49%) visiting at least one protected area in 2016. Thus, the value of these natural ecosystems for tourism is already significant. Well managed nature tourism can bring much needed revenues to Peru's protected areas as well as employment opportunities for local people, and, in some areas, it can counteract deforestation by outcompeting alternative uses of forested land in terms of the economic benefits generated from marketable products. Due to their charisma, size, and relative ease of observation giant otters represent a precious asset to the nature tourism industry. Already, more than 50,000 international tourists per year travel to Madre de Dios in the hope of observing giant otters in the wild.

Giant otters also have instrumental value in the sense that we can use them as biodiversity management and ecosystem conservation tools. The giant otter is an apex predator requiring highly productive aquatic habitats and its population status reflects the structure, function, and overall health of riverine ecosystems. They can therefore be regarded as good ecological indicators, for example, for tourism management. Furthermore, the species can serve as a central character for environmental education activities, and as a flagship or ambassador for communication and conservation campaigns. The fact giant otter families share

Nature tourism is booming in several regions of the giant otter's distribution range. (JG)

several valued traits with human families — joint care of siblings, a love of play, strong partner loyalty, and others — can be useful in helping to bridge the enormous empathy gap that still exists between man and other non-human animals.

GOALS FOR GIANT OTTER CONSERVATION

Using demographic and behavioural data from the giant otter population of the Manu River floodplain, a simulation model was developed to investigate its dynamics. The model demonstrated that the two most critical variables for achieving giant otter population persistence are the number of breeding groups and the number of dispersing, sexually mature individuals. The model allowed us to calculate the likelihood of a transient otter meeting a potential mate in a suitable, vacant territory within a limited time. First, there must be a reasonable number of transients in a given aquatic habitat. The greater the number of dispersers in the population the sooner the empty territory is colonised. If the number of dispersers sinks below a certain threshold, the probability of encounter is reduced and with it the likelihood that new families will be founded. This may result in a self-perpetuating downward trend that eventually leads to the extinction of a local population.

Second, the number of breeding groups must be sufficient to provide a minimum number of dispersers each year. Thus, below a critical number of groups, the chances of colonisation drop dramatically. The model showed that local events which reduce

The persistence of otter populations is strongly influenced by the ability of dispersers to move through the landscape. (FH)

Giant otter population persistence in relation to the number of dispersers in the population

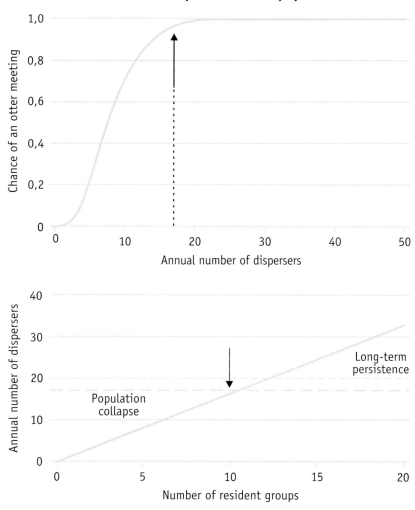

the number of dispersing otters, such as decreased reproductive success as a result of poorly managed tourism, could potentially destabilize the population. Recovery from such events can take several years, especially in a population that is already struggling. Maximising the number of breeding groups in a given population, thereby enhancing the colonisation potential of its transients, is a key goal for giant otter conservation.

We believe giant otters historically occurred in the entire Madre de Dios watershed up to an altitude of roughly 600 metres above sea level. It would be foolhardy, however, to set out to manage aquatic habitats below 600 metres and forget about the conservation of headwater habitats. Cloud and montane forests in the headwaters are crucial for maintaining the hydrological balance of the watershed and many species of fish, some of which are key prey species of the otters, depend on the headwaters for spawning. Pollution, dam construction, invasive species, and poor management of headwaters will all ultimately affect downstream habitats and hence the giant otter. A watershed approach is therefore essential for giant otter conservation, in Peru and elsewhere.

One of the most important conclusions arising from our giant otter research and population monitoring is that large floodplain oxbow lakes make good quality habitat for giant otters. These lakes tend to be occupied by large otter groups and have higher cub productivity because the number of helpers is larger, litters are larger, and cub survival is higher. As a result, large lakes produce more dispersers and more of these dispersers are successful in founding new groups elsewhere and raising a litter of cubs of their own.

Considerations of source-sink dynamics are important to inform conservation management decisions, especially when planning the creation or expansion of protected areas. Source habitats are those where local reproductive success is greater than local mortality. Populations in source habitats produce an excess of individuals, which must disperse outside their natal area to settle and breed. Sink habitats are areas where local otter productivity is lower than local mortality. Without immigration from other areas, populations in sink habitats will inevitably spiral into extinction.

Thus, floodplains with large lakes may potentially act as source habitats for the species – the larger the oxbow lake, the higher its value as source habitat – while

An oxbow lake in the making. In south-eastern Peru, large, undisturbed oxbows are vital for the long-term survival of local giant otter populations and may act as source habitats. (WW)

headwater rivers and smaller rainforest streams are likely to be sink habitats. Reproductive success per group is approximately three times higher on large oxbow lakes than that of giant otter families living on small rivers, while survival to dispersal age is also higher on the lakes. Special care must therefore be taken to safeguard source habitats. As a minimum, floodplain forests immediately surrounding lakes, as well as the small streams that drain them, should also be protected since these play a crucial role in the lake food chain, especially during the rainy season when fish enter the flooded swamp and forest areas to feed. Many fish species inhabiting Madre de Dios lakes are specialized insect, fruit, and seed eaters, while another large proportion feeds on detritus resulting in great part from organic matter from the forest. In other parts of the species range where large lakes are absent, other habitat features may define what makes good quality source habitat.

HOW DO WE GO ABOUT IT?

Conservation management must be both participative and adaptive in order to be effective. It must be participative because as researchers we only hold part of the knowledge needed for successful conservation; local economic and social know-how is also essential. Moreover, conservation depends to a large extent on local actors for its sustainability, and without the meaningful involvement of tourism operators, native people, or local fishermen in the planning stages, it is unlikely they will prove to be strong allies during implementation. In protected areas, involving park guards is essential as they have continuous presence and can implement and monitor activities on a day-to-day basis.

Management must also be adaptive; we must learn systematically from our successes and failures. Adaptive management is key because, firstly, giant otter conservation takes place in tropical forests — complex, dynamic systems often occupied by human populations of multiple cultural origins practising multiple extractive activities. Continuous learning is one way in which we can deal with this complexity. Secondly, giant otter conservation occurs in a constantly changing world. Logging companies adopt new tactics to reach remaining stands of mahogany and other precious hardwoods. Gold miners form associations and lobby politicians so they can continue mining where they should not. Oil companies react to increasing oil and gas prices and pull strings in order to weaken conservation laws so they can enter protected areas. As society and nature constantly change, so must conservation projects be flexible and adapt accordingly. And finally, giant otter conservation must advance, even in the face of incomplete information. We need to act now, together with protected area managers, community conservation groups, student bodies, and others, or we will continue to lag behind. Miners will not stop mining, loggers will not stop logging, and human populations will not stop growing for many years to come.

Habitat zoning and the management of human activities

While sitting at dawn on the bank of Cocha Brasco, watching a group of six giant otters coming out of their den on the opposite shore, it was difficult to believe what Zacarias was telling us; that less than 30 years ago the Brasco family operated the largest sawmill of the Manu River at precisely this spot. Back then, the lake was still a meander of the river and thousands of Spanish cedar trees growing on the floodplain were felled and floated down to this point to be sawn. Nothing remains of the mill today; the only telltale sign it ever existed is the complete lack of large cedars along the banks of the lake. The young cedars that have grown since its formation appear insignificant when compared to the metre-wide giants that are typical further upriver in areas loggers never reached.

This experience exemplifies how riverine and floodplain habitats can recover from the incursion of man, given the chance. In 1968, thanks in great part to the work of Peruvian taxonomist and conservationist, Celestino Kalinowski, and British naturalist, Ian Grimwood, a large proportion of the Manu River watershed was set aside for conservation. Kalinowski, who had worked in the area for more than twenty years, travelled deep into Manu with Grimwood in 1967. Grimwood had been invited by the Peruvian government to locate the site for Peru's first Amazonian park. On his return to Lima, Grimwood wrote 'Manu is *the* place for a Park – beyond a shadow of

Explaining the importance of protected areas should begin at school. Habits and lifestyles are, at least in part, developed early in life. By focusing on children, environmental education may succeed in reaching into their homes and their families. (FH)

a doubt.' The area was formally declared a National Park in 1973 and all logging in the Manu watershed came to a halt within two years of the Park's creation, thanks to the work of a handful of dedicated conservationists and park guards.

Zoning is a popular planning tool in varied fields, from urban development, to fisheries, to conservation. Zoning makes explicit where and under what conditions activities can take place in a defined area. It is especially useful when human groups with different priorities are using a shared and/or scarce resource. The creation and expansion of protected areas is an example of habitat zoning at the landscape level. When backed by legislation as well as adequate control and management measures, protected areas become one of the cornerstones of our efforts to safeguard biodiversity.

In the case of carnivores, their trophic position constrains them to living at low population densities and their diet often brings them into conflict with local people who share their affinity for meat and fish. Large protected areas are therefore crucial for carnivores, both in order to ensure demographically viable populations and to reduce carnivore-people conflict. This is especially true for giant otters in

Habitat zoning at different spatial scales

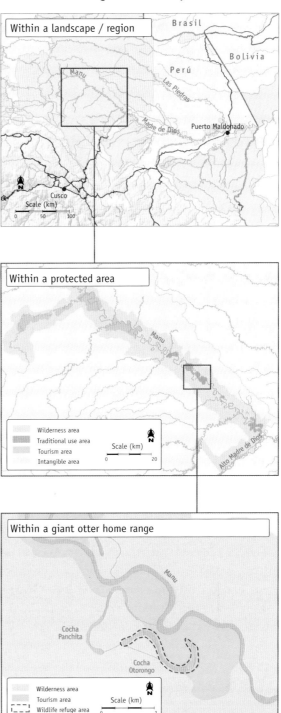

Madre de Dios. Their aquatic habitats cover less than 1% of the total rainforest area of the region and although found at relatively high local densities in their preferred habitat, oxbow lakes, their total densities are much lower than those of other large predators such as jaguars and pumas. Their prey, fish, is also a highly valued and important source of protein for local people, natives and immigrants alike. In Madre de Dios, conflict over fisheries has so far not been significant because the otters are found in remote areas with low human densities. However, in a scenario of species recovery and growing human populations, it is likely that this conflict would increase as has been the case in other parts of Peru and further afield.

There has been great progress in the establishment of protected areas in Madre de Dios: Manu National Park in 1973; Pampas del Heath National Sanctuary in 1983; Bahuaja Sonene National Park and Tambopata National Reserve in 2000; Amarakaeri Communal Reserve in 2002; and Alto Purus National Park in 2004. The latter covers more than 2.5 million hectares, including around 600,000 hectares in the headwaters of the Las Piedras River. Oxbow lakes are small but plentiful in the meandering upper reaches of the Las Piedras, providing important habitat for giant otters. Together, these protected areas encompass a total of over 5.3 million hectares under non-consumptive use and 650,000 hectares under managed consumptive use.

Expansion of existing protected areas in order to include high quality giant otter source habitats is also an important strategy. This occurred in Manu, where the definitive step for giant otters came in 2002, when the Reserved Zone (declared in 1980) and an as yet unprotected portion of the Pinquen River, one of Manu's most important tributaries, were formally incorporated into the National Park, adding over 200,000 hectares and a large part of the Manu floodplain. Although only representing a 12% surface extension, this area has consistently harboured more than 60% of the local otter population. However, efforts to protect the biodiversity of the Amazon have generally focused on the creation and maintenance of a network of protected areas with intact forests as important conservation objects, supported by policies in all Amazonian countries. Rivers and their watersheds are often not specifically considered in protected area design or management.

Peru's Protected Area Law also enables regional authorities, communities, and private owners to establish protected areas. To date, 18 regional conservation areas and 122 private conservation areas have been established in the country. In a complementary fashion, Peru's Forestry and Wildlife Law enables the state to award conservation, ecotourism, and forestry concessions in order to stimulate the involvement of nongovernmental organizations and the business sector in conservation, thereby counteracting informal colonisation and illegal activities. The giant otter population of the Los Amigos River increased slowly thanks in large part to the creation, in 2001, of the 136,000 hectare Amigos River Conservation Concession which covers the lower watershed of the Los Amigos River and is managed by the

Amazon Conservation Association. The re-colonisation by giant otters of the Madre de Dios floodplain lakes near the mouth of this river is a significant step forward in the local recovery of the species. Thus far, 16 conservation concessions, totalling over 192,000 hectares, and 14 ecotourism concessions, totalling just over 21,000 hectares, have been awarded in Madre de Dios. This is an exciting development for giant otter conservation in areas where the establishment of large protected areas is no longer realistic.

Creation of protected areas, then, is an example of zoning at the landscape level, a level directly relevant to giant otter populations. However, many of these protected areas are very large and zoning of each area is necessary in order to facilitate management. Even in National Parks, where giant otters are in theory afforded complete protection, most human activities are concentrated on water bodies and areas of forest immediately surrounding them. Subsistence fishing and agriculture by native people; tourism infrastructure and excursions; transport by researchers, park staff, locals and tourists alike; all take place to a great extent along rivers and in lakes. Protected area zoning is a first step in the management of these specific threats and acts at the level of giant otter sub-populations.

Seven zoning categories currently exist within the Peruvian protected area system: Strict Protection, Wilderness, Tourism and Recreation, Traditional Use, Restoration, Historic-Cultural, and Direct Use. Zoning of a protected area should be compatible with the conservation objectives and protection level of the area. For example, it makes sense that in a Communal Reserve a larger percentage of habitat is zoned for Traditional Use – subsistence fishing for example – than in a National Park, while in a National Reserve a Direct Use Zone may include managed commercial fisheries. By the same token, the Tourism and Recreation Zone in a Scenic or National Reserve will be larger than in a National Park, where the emphasis will be on attracting smaller, low impact visitor groups.

In 2002, the Manu floodplain was zoned into three of the above categories: traditional use, wilderness, and tourism and recreation. Traditional use zones are areas occupied by native communities that pre-date the establishment of the protected area. In these areas traditional forms of resource use may continue. Wilderness zones are areas with little or no human intervention, where monitoring, research and control activities predominate. Restricted education and tourism activities may be undertaken, but no infrastructure or motorized transport is permitted.

Of the 12 giant otter family territories identified within the zoned area as a whole, four are located within the tourism and recreation zone, two in the Matsigenka traditional use zone, and six in the wilderness zone. The basic conservation concept here is that by having the giant otter population spread over a variety of use areas, the threat to the population represented by any specific anthropogenic effect is diminished. For example, if the human population inhabiting the park increases over the coming decades and the intensity of subsistence fishing increases to a level where fish stocks are compromised, only two of the otter groups in the floodplain, 15% of the population, would be threatened by this development. An increase in the human population density of the park would, of course, lead to myriad effects on its integrity, possibly even leading to pressures to re-zone the area, but that does not invalidate current zoning efforts.

Resident family groups form the bulk of giant otter populations. In Madre de Dios, these groups inhabit territories that are relatively small and stable over time. At the core of many higher quality territories, ones which support larger groups with higher reproductive success, is a large oxbow lake. Such oxbow lakes are not only important for the otters, they are also key nesting and feeding habitat for a wealth of other wildlife. Furthermore, due to their high fish productivity and scenic beauty, lakes are favoured destinations of fishermen and tourists respectively. Zoning of oxbow lakes is part of the effort to manage these activities and is therefore a tool for the conservation of specific resident giant otter groups.

Behavioural and habitat studies in Madre de Dios have shed light on which factors are important for the wellbeing of giant otter groups. One of the most important is that they need disturbance-free areas on riverine shores for constructing dens and raising their cubs. To ensure this, paths along shores should be diverted and important denning sites should be included in the refuge areas on the lake itself. Most groups have two or three dens situated in high bank areas of the shore that are critical to successful breeding. These dens should be included in the no-go areas.

The giant otter's innate anti-predator behaviour on encountering a boat is frequently misunderstood. It is revealing how often we have been told by Madre de Dios fishermen and guides that the otters were 'very tame' or 'they came to say hello.' In areas where otters are routinely chased, they learn to view boats as 'super predators' that are not intimidated by their usual warning behaviour. This results in changes in otter behaviour and habitat use patterns. In contrast, otters habituate relatively quickly to fixed observation points on the shore. Even groups with young can be seen fishing a mere twenty metres from platforms and observation hides. It is possible that the contrast in how otters habituate to boats and fixed infrastructure can be explained by the difference in the ability of the otters to predict the 'threat' and their freedom of action in either situation. In the case of stationary points on the shore, the otter group is able to choose whether or not to seek out a particular area, adjusting gradually to the disturbance, which remains constant and local and is thus predictable. In comparison, otters are often surprised by boats which are mobile and can appear suddenly in the vicinity of dens. Otters are unable to foresee the locations or times of boat disturbances. Fixed observation points such as hides and towers are therefore one of the tools for lower impact giant otter viewing.

THE GIANT OTTER

Amazon tourism concentrates along rivers and lakes, almost completely overlapping giant otter habitat. (JMR)

Finally, giant otters thrive on high densities of fish. For this reason, it is important that no destructive fishing methods — dynamite, poisons, or nets with too fine a mesh — are used on oxbow lakes. Avoiding lake contamination and the destruction of floating, shoreline, and floodplain vegetation is necessary in order to preserve the food chains on which fish depend. Studies carried out to date show that fish populations of lakes are highly dynamic and that, depending on water levels and the time of year, there is much movement of fish between lakes and main river channels. It is therefore important not to allow fishing with nets across channels connecting lakes to the river, as they may prevent re-population of the former and vice versa.

Three different zoning categories are proposed for oxbow lakes. Refuge Areas are established around fragile areas or locations of high conservation priority. In the case of giant otters, key denning, marking, and resting sites should be included in the Refuge Area. No infrastructure or human visitation is permitted, with the exception of research, monitoring, or control activities authorised by the institution managing the lake. The benefits of refuge or no-go areas in fisheries is already well documented, both for biodiversity and for the profitability of the fisheries themselves. On the other end of the scale are Consumptive Use Areas, established in areas of lower conservation priority that can sustain extractive activities such as commercial fisheries.

Zoning concept

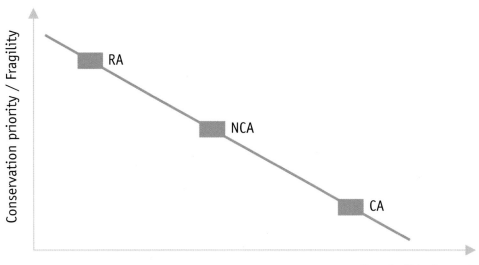

RA: Refuge Area
NCA: Non-consumptive Use Area
CA: Consumptive Use Area

Infrastructure should be concentrated in these areas. Non-consumptive Use Areas are the third category and can serve as a buffer between Refuge and Consumptive Use Areas. Priority is given to tourism, recreation, and education activities, and to the implementation of appropriate codes of conduct and operation standards for these activities. Access to certain places can be regulated, for example, by means of the visitor capacity of infrastructure (observation tower, hide, etc).

Zoning of lakes must also consider what happens in adjacent land areas, as the integrity of floodplain forests and wetlands surrounding the lakes is essential for maintaining their fisheries and wildlife value. Activities that imply the removal of forest cover, such as logging and gold mining, should therefore be excluded from these areas. Micro-watersheds that feed the lake must be protected in their entirety.

An important principle in order for different interest groups (conservationists, tourist operators, fishermen, and native people alike) to adopt the zoning plans is proportionality with regards to the human use patterns of the wider habitat matrix in which the lake is embedded. For example, the zoning of a lake in a National Park will be weighted in favour of Refuge Areas while the zoning of a lake in an area dedicated to fisheries will favour the creation of consumptive use areas. As mentioned earlier, conservation takes place in complex, changing environments and the following table can only be used as a guideline that should be adapted to local circumstances:

ZONING GUIDELINES FOR OXBOW LAKES

Item	Non-consumptive Use protected area (i.e. National Park)	Consumptive Use protected area (i.e. National Reserve) or buffer areas	Non protected area (Matrix habitat)
Refuge Area: size and activities	60% of lake, includes 100 metre strip of shoreline forest. No human use except essential monitoring and control activities.	40% of lake, including 100 metre strip of shoreline forest. No human use except essential monitoring and control activities.	20% of lake, including 100 metre strip of shoreline forest. No human use except essential monitoring and control activities.
Non-consumptive Use Area: size and activities	Remaining 40% of lake. Education, accompanied by qualified teacher. Nature tourism and recreation, accompanied by certified naturalist guides. No fishing, including sport fishing.	30% of lake. Education and recreation, accompanied by qualified teacher. Nature tourism, accompanied by certified naturalist guides. No motorized transport.	30% of lake. Nature tourism, education and recreation. Catch and release sport fishing.
Consumptive Use Area: size and activities	Not applicable*	30% of lake. Sport fishing, local or commercial fisheries following approved management plan.	50% of lake. Sport fishing, local or commercial fisheries.
Infrastructure	No housing or tourism infrastructure on lake shores, except access platforms and viewing facilities.	All infrastructure concentrated away from Refuge Area. Minimize shoreline development.	All infrastructure concentrated away from Refuge Area. Minimize shoreline development.
Boats	No motors. Replace single hull with double hull boats in order to concentrate visitors. Observation towers and hides as alternatives to boats for viewing wildlife.	Preferentially boats without motors. Replace combustion motors with electric motors. Towers and hides as alternatives to boats for viewing wildlife.	Minimize use of motorized transport where possible.
Paths	At 100 metres from shoreline all around lake.	At 100 metres from shoreline in Refuge Area of lake	At 100 metres from shoreline in Refuge Area of lake.
Riparian Vegetation	No clearing of forest along shore.	Minimum clearing of forest along shore.	Minimum clearing of forest along shore.

*Except in lakes where traditional fishing by native people takes place. In this case an area should be zoned specifically for this activity.

Where should the burden of proof lie?

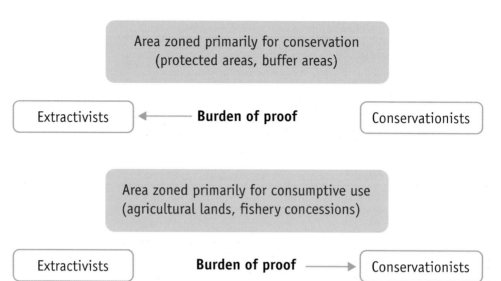

A final concept regarding the zoning and management of lakes involves burden of proof. Obviously, giant otters cannot lobby in defence of their needs in the same way a tourist operator or a fishermen association can. But on whose shoulders should the burden of proof rest? Is it the conservationist's responsibility to prove that giant otter wellbeing will be compromised if a certain resource use activity goes ahead or is it the developer's or resource user's responsibility to prove that their activity will not harm the giant otters? Although fundamentally an ethical question, a pragmatic answer could be to propose that the burden of proof lies with the developers in areas zoned primarily for giant otter and biodiversity conservation, and with conservationists in areas zoned primarily for consumptive use.

Tourism Management

The management of tourism in relation to giant otters deserves special attention, in part because tourism is the main economic activity currently being promoted in protected areas, often strongholds for giant otters, and in other rural areas to mitigate giant otter-fisherman conflict. Experience in Peru has shown that tourism and giant otters can co-exist harmoniously, even thrive together, if the former is managed to respect the needs of the latter. Giant otters favour large oxbow lakes with plenty of fish and high, path-free shorelines for building dens and latrines. If tourism could take these habitat requirements into account, not only would giant otters benefit by being able to lead uninterrupted lives, their cubs safe, but our chances of observing these wonderful animals for long periods in their natural habitat would be

Well managed tourism that is sensitive to the needs of giant otters can be an effective conservation tool. (JG)

greatly increased since they would feel at ease in our presence. Such an extraordinary experience would bring us back to the rainforest time and again.

So what can we do as responsible guides, tour operators, and tourists? By learning to interpret otter behaviour and giving them space we can reduce the risks of disturbing them. Certified guides should inform themselves about giant otter biology and behaviour, participate in tourist guide training opportunities, and take responsibility for educating tourists about protected area regulations, their own potential impact on otters, and proper conduct. When giant otter viewing is carried out from boats, a minimum observation distance of 50 metres between us and the otters should be maintained, and binoculars and telescopes should be used to improve the quality of observation. The use of double hull canoes, or catamarans, provides greater stability and therefore better viewing and photographic opportunities. They can also accommodate larger groups of tourists, thereby reducing boat traffic, and move slower than single-hulled canoes, making it harder to chase the otters. A booking system can be implemented that limits excursions to time slots of a maximum time period. The catamaran should be rowed along a fixed route that respects the refuge area.

Tourism operators should not construct lodges directly on lake shores and paths should be cleared away from the shoreline, at least 50 metres inland. In addition to

Scenic views and excellent wildlife observations are possible from towers and hides. In some areas, giant otters may habituate more easily to fixed observation points than to moving boats. (FH)

An habituated otter that has recently separated from its natal group sniffs curiously at our oar. (FH)

developing alternatives to lake excursions, low impact observation points such as hides and towers should replace boats where feasible. Tourists should expect their guide and tour operator to stick to the above recommendations and choose tour operators that have a proven nature conservation record.

Provided we understand and accept that, like us, giant otters need space and tranquillity, especially during the breeding season, tourism and giant otter conservation can be compatible. The above zoning principles have been applied in eight different oxbow lakes in Madre de Dios. Specific tourism management activities have been undertaken in six of these eight lakes. Monitoring of giant otter groups before and after implementation of management zoning has shown that reproductive success on unmanaged lakes is significantly lower than that on managed lakes. Reproductive success on managed lakes is slightly lower than reproductive success on lakes where no human activities take place, but the difference is not significant. Following are two case studies that exemplify the local realities and management steps taken to improve both the tourism experience as well as the wellbeing of the resident otter families.

Lake Sandoval, with an open water surface area of 125 hectares, is the largest oxbow lake in the Tambopata National Reserve. It is surrounded by a beautiful Mauritia palm swamp and is only half an hour by boat from Puerto Maldonado, the capital of Madre de Dios. Having been the site for experimental fish farming of paiche (*Arapaima gigas*) in the 1960s, the lake is now principally used for tourism and small-scale, commercial, and subsistence fishing.

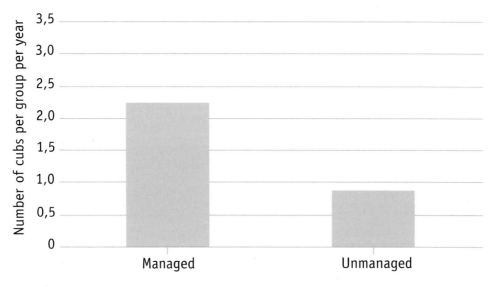

Average giant otter reproductive success in managed versus unmanaged lakes

THE GIANT OTTER

There are two lodges on the lake; one is run by a local family and attracts budget travellers, and the other is aimed at wealthier nature tourists. Several other tourism operators as well as freelance guides bring a total of roughly 20,000 tourists per year to the lake. In 1999, a participative management process, led by the Frankfurt Zoological Society, was initiated in order to solve some of the more pressing problems in the area, including illegal hunting and wood extraction, chaotic school excursions, open disputes between tourism operators, unauthorised construction of tourism infrastructure, and reduced reproductive success of the resident giant otter group. This participative process led to several management actions, including the construction of the Sandoval Control Post and Interpretation Centre in 2002 and 2003 respectively, development of a structured environmental education programme since 2002, implementation of a wildlife sightings monitoring programme since 2003, and improved maintenance of shared infrastructure.

Park guards, here in the Lake Sandoval Interpretation Centre, are often armed with detailed local knowledge and can be valuable allies in protected area zoning. (FH)

Local residents on Lake Sandoval became strong supporters of the development of a site-specific management plan. (FH)

Lake Sandoval before and after management zoning

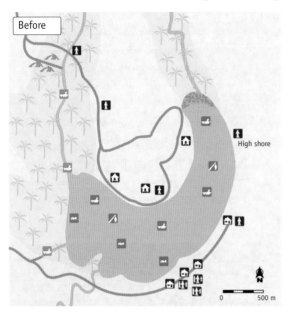

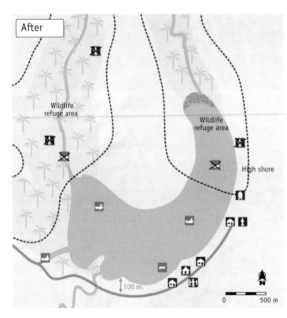

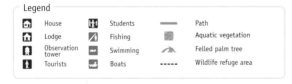

Legend

🏠	House	👫	Students	—	Path	
🏠	Lodge	▨	Fishing	▨	Aquatic vegetation	
🏠	Observation tower	▬	Swimming	⌂	Felled palm tree	
🏠	Tourists	▬	Boats	-----	Wildlife refuge area	

An important milestone was the implementation of a formal zoning and site management plan in 2004, the first such example in the Peruvian Protected Area System. The main challenges in Sandoval involved building trust with the local people and tourism operators and developing management capacity within the Reserve. In the beginning, several tourism operators failed to participate because they believed there was a hidden agenda to benefit one of the other operators. Local people were hesitant because they viewed the project as a tourism interest itself. To be, and be seen, as impartial and professional was vital. Reserve authorities hired and trained additional park guards to man the Control Post and maintain an ongoing dialogue with all actors. As a result of these actions, in 2006, Sandoval generated about 60% of tourism income of the Reserve, giant otter reproductive success increased, and otter sighting success by visitors nearly tripled between 2003 and 2005.

Tres Chimbadas is a 55 hectare oxbow lake in the buffer area of the Tambopata National Reserve. Since 2000, two tourism operators have followed a voluntary management plan on the lake. In a nutshell, management until 2004 involved respecting a wildlife Refuge Area on the lake, training all guides in wildlife observation guidelines, and following a fixed route during the

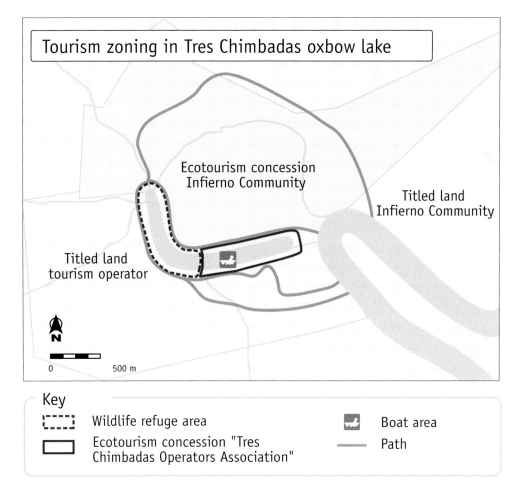

Tourism zoning in Tres Chimbadas oxbow lake

Ecotourism concession
Infierno Community

Titled land
Infierno Community

Titled land
tourism operator

N

0   500 m

Key

┌╌╌╌┐
└╌╌╌┘   Wildlife refuge area   🛶 Boat area

┌───┐   Ecotourism concession "Tres   ------ Path
└───┘   Chimbadas Operators Association"

canoe excursions on the open part of the lake. Advancing agricultural pressure to the north west of the lake and the arrival, during 2004, of an operator who was not willing to adopt the voluntary management guidelines set by the first two companies, catalysed a management formalisation process. The latter involved clarifying legal land tenure for all actors in the area of influence of the lake, including the native community of Infierno, part owner of one of the tourist operations. Once there was clarity regarding land tenure, we supported the Infierno community in obtaining an ecotourism concession on the north side of the lake. The strategy was to create a continuous strip of land around the lake, dedicated to managed nature tourism activities, which would act as a buffer to agriculture, commercial fisheries, and mismanaged tourism. The last step was to set up a tourism operator association to request a tourism concession encompassing the lake itself and the 50-metre strip of forest all around the shoreline. Management responsibility was then delegated by the State to the concession holders, according to an approved management plan.

Average giant otter sighting success by tourist groups on managed and unmanaged lakes

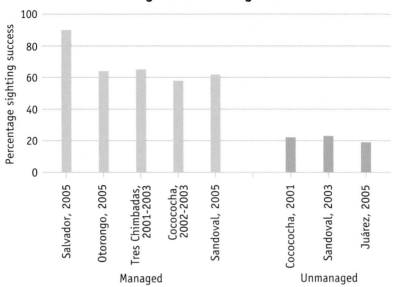

Monthly giant otter sighting success by tourist groups on a managed and unmanaged lake

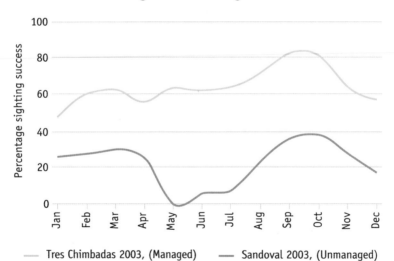

— Tres Chimbadas 2003, (Managed)   — Sandoval 2003, (Unmanaged)

In Tres Chimbadas, observation success peaks during the breeding season showing that the group feels at ease with its cubs on the lake. In Sandoval, until 2003, the otter family took its cubs to the Mauritia palm swamp, a sub-optimal habitat, and sighting success decreased markedly.

Many native and settler communities in Madre de Dios and in other parts of the giant otter's range want to work in nature tourism and have high expectations of the results. We have seen several examples of local people who invested all they own in an outboard motor, in the hope of transporting tourists, or in a small, self-built lodge, only to find later that the tourism industry is much more complicated and fickle than they imagined. Most of these initiatives have quickly failed, even those that received substantial outside support. A successful tourism business takes management skills, know-how, and contacts that most local people can only dream of having. For local tourism initiatives to be successful, therefore, innovative, long-term alliances with the business and development sector will need to be forged.

Training and capacity-building

Over the years we conducted many courses for tourism guides, tourism operators, and park guards on the theme of giant otters and their conservation. These covered simple subjects like basic ecology and giant otter identification, to more complex issues such as the design of site-specific management plans. Most were organised in the field, in Control Posts and lodges: we were thus able to keep the courses practical and focused on the conservation of the resident groups of otters living nearby. When addressing

Tailored training courses for tourism guides and park guards are important for the successful management of human activities in giant otter habitats. (FH)

habitat management, we have time and again observed the importance of not telling people how to go about protecting the otters, but rather provide background information as well as conservation tools and ideas, and then motivate participants to present and debate amongst themselves their management proposals. Armed with information about the giant otter's needs as well as knowledge of the local realities and constraints, local actors will often arrive at management solutions best suited to the local setting. Fostering a sense of ownership of, and empathy for, the otter groups and their wellbeing is fundamental to site management planning and has probably been the most valuable outcome of these training efforts.

Education and awareness-raising

The attitude of many people towards giant otters and other wildlife is frequently one of ignorance, or one that says wildlife exists to be consumed. The possibility of local extinction through overexploitation is often not considered at all or is shrugged off as irrelevant and there is a general lack of concern about implications for the future. The concept of conservation is sometimes not one that is familiar, or understood, or taken seriously. This attitude stems partly from a feeling of complacency and partly from a lack of education.

It's a cliché nowadays but undeniably true; we only protect what we love and we only love what we know. For those of us who have had the good fortune to grow up experiencing wildlife it is difficult to understand the indifference that many people express towards nature. A large proportion of South Americans living in cities and towns, even those in the rainforest, have little opportunity to experience nature first-hand, while for much of the remaining rural population the pressing struggle of day-to-day life precludes an appreciation of nature. The resulting negative human perceptions – that giant otters are dangerous, cubs make fun pets, and populations are growing exponentially – can only be modified by communication of the facts obtained through objective research. The importance of environmental education as a conservation tool is often underestimated, yet it is key to influencing human behaviours, with positive outcomes such as reducing human wildlife conflicts and promoting the conservation of biodiversity.

Pepe, the Giant Otter

Conservation education campaigns have done much to raise awareness and build a strong base of social support for giant otter conservation in Madre de Dios. Between 1998 and 2005, the Frankfurt Zoological Society engaged 13,400 children aged six to eight years old, and more than 300 teachers, in a colouring book activity and competition, *Pepe, the Giant Otter*, designed to raise awareness about giant otter conservation. Key aspects of giant otter behaviour and ecology were illustrated in the booklet, on the basis of their appeal to young children as well as their importance in contributing towards a first understanding of rainforest preservation. All children earned prizes in special ceremonies, with the best drawings receiving additional recognition in the form of school materials. The enjoyment expressed by these children and the high response rate to the drawing competitions suggest that such an activity can play a significant role in raising conservation awareness amongst local communities.

Proper follow-up of the material distribution, colouring, and drawing competition process is necessary to ensure the motivation of participating teachers, who are key allies in this activity. To this effect, a teachers' manual was prepared in which they are encouraged to carry out different educational activities with each drawing.

Children's inherent interest in nature is brought to life with Pepe. (CA)

Using a page of the book showing several different otters and other animals, basic addition and subtraction is covered. Another page is used to explore the concept of colours, while a third page illustrating an otter family is used to discuss how we can be helpful in our own families. The most satisfying part of working with Pepe has been arriving at schools and being received by impromptu giant otter puppet shows, songs, and murals, all prepared by the teachers and their pupils. Translated and adapted versions of *Pepe, the Giant Otter* have also been used in environmental education campaigns implemented in French Guiana and Brazil.

Tito intiri Chavaropana

More recently, an illustrated conservation education booklet was created by San Diego Zoo Global Peru for the Matsigenka communities in and around Manu, in Matsigenka and Spanish, and funded through the Wildlife Conservation Research Unit (WildCRU-University of Oxford). The main protagonists are a Matsigenka boy, Tito, acting as the voice of his community and a young giant otter, Chava, representing the flagship species of the aquatic environment in particular, and of Manu National Park as a whole. The illustrated story, co-authored by a Matsigenka community leader, explores the worlds and perspectives of each, blending Matsigenka folklore with natural history and key conservation messages. About 2,000 copies of the booklet are currently being distributed among Matsigenka families in the Manu region and its impact on school children is being evaluated. This study will guide the text and message of a second book in the series, again to be published with the support of WildCRU.

Different actors — tourists, school children, the general public — can be addressed with a range of communication tools, from leaflets, articles, and books to posters and TV documentaries, to bring home the message of giant otter conservation.

A Walk to Lake Sandoval

As part of the zoning and management of Lake Sandoval, the programme *A Walk to Lake Sandoval* was initiated in 2002, in response to the need of the Tambopata National Reserve to reduce conflicts arising from chaotic school excursions to the area. During the months of August and September, roughly 1,500 children would visit the lake, in groups of up to 300 students, with only one or two teachers supervising. The resulting noise, rubbish, and general disturbance diminished the quality of the experience for other visitors to the area; August and September are also the peak tourism months.

It was decided to spread school visits throughout the year, and to reduce maximum group size to 30 children. The learning value of visits was increased by having preparatory as well as post visit classes in all schools. *A Walk to Sandoval* became not just a fun field day out, but an intensive encounter with nature, during which children learned to identify animals and habitats, to become aware of their own small impact on nature, and to accept prudent distances for wildlife observation. A total of 30 local higher education student volunteers acted as assistant guides, helping the programme environmental educator and the teachers to manage the children. The student

While international tourism is important, the experience of nature by local people, especially children, is even more so.

volunteers not only increased their knowledge of education, tourism, and conservation, but also gained valuable leadership skills. The importance of multipliers cannot be over-emphasised; it helps if the education message reaches an audience which can then itself spread the message further. Educating teachers and key personnel in protected area management are good examples of this.

The programme allowed Reserve authorities to enrich visits of the local students and to reduce conflicts with other users of the lake. More than 3,200 students, 120 teachers, and 15 schools participated. The Head of Tambopata National Reserve and the park guards not only supported and participated in the programme, but also used it as a model for a wider environmental education circuit for the protected area, in which several education-oriented nongovernmental organisations and the regional branch of the Ministry of Education became involved. The students themselves covered roughly 50% of travel costs, thereby contributing to the sustainability of the activities.

Both *Pepe, the Giant Otter* and *A Walk to Lake Sandoval* were effective in creating goodwill amongst parents and local authorities. In fact, the encouraging response to these activities, as well as openness by the local government to include a much stronger nature and environmental component in the regional curricula, indicated that education is probably one of the best ways of building a strong base of social support for conservation in Madre de Dios. The introduction of giant otter biology and conservation information into private and state school texts was also heartening evidence that giant otters can play a role in the wider education context.

Communication

Twenty-five years ago most people in Peru had never heard of the giant otter. Many films, booklets, articles, and radio interviews later we can safely say that basic awareness of the species at a national level has grown. But how many people are aware that National Parks in Madre de Dios are playing a crucial role in their protection or that tourism must be adequately managed in order to become a force for giant otter conservation? In a world flooded with information, it is difficult to assess how best to continue communicating the needs of giant otter conservation and the lessons learnt. It is a fact of present-day society that people are more susceptible to images than words, especially in the case of children who are growing up in a world dominated by television and the Internet. In this sense, photographs, videos, social media, and websites become important instruments for transmitting the giant otter conservation message. Distributing relevant information at the local, rural level, in the form of printed leaflets and booklets, has also proven to be effective in raising awareness. This is because many areas of Madre de Dios have only recently gained access to the Internet and other mass media and many people still like to possess a hard copy of information which they can take home and share with their families.

One of the most important of communication tasks is surely to convey the message that the survival of giant otter populations depends on maintaining the ecological integrity of watersheds. Satisfying basic needs and the justified aspirations for a better quality of life of the people of Amazonia must be achieved without significantly damaging the continued capacity of aquatic ecosystems to provide services and natural landscapes for the benefit of man and other non-human species.

Population monitoring

The incorporation of research findings and field data into conservation action is one of the keystones of adaptive management. We cannot pretend effectively to manage giant otter populations without reliable monitoring data. Without this data we would not be able to chart the recovery or decline of giant otter populations, nor would we be able to make population estimates over larger areas, essential for prioritizing and implementing conservation measures. We would not be able to gauge the impact that fisheries or tourism have on the behaviour or reproductive success of giant otter groups or the effectiveness of implemented management actions. Distribution and population data collected in a standardised format and following an established census protocol can provide reliable, comparable, and user-friendly data on which to base conservation decisions.

FURTHER RESEARCH

Over the years of giant otter observation, many intriguing questions have surfaced, the answers to which would greatly enhance our understanding of giant otter ecology. In fact, the more we learn, the more we wonder. Unfortunately, the most interesting may be the most difficult to address. For example, we know very little about the nature and relative importance of natural mortality factors such as predation and disease. Incredibly, during years of research in Madre de Dios, we found only one dead giant otter, a decomposing newborn cub at the entrance of a den. We are aware that cub mortality is high but can only guess at the causes.

We now know a little about the ecology and behaviour of giant otter groups. However, we know almost nothing of the spacing behaviour and movement patterns of transients once they have left their families. Where do they go, how far do they travel, do they frequently disperse across watersheds as well as along them? What threats do they face, how do they integrate into existing groups, and how are new groups formed? Radio telemetry in the rainforest is hampered by local conditions: we need to devise innovative ways of tracking giant otters in the field. Camera traps, for example, are a less invasive tool for obtaining throat markings, and for obtaining information on sex, approximate age, and reproductive status not easily available from direct observation.

Continuity in giant otter research and monitoring is essential for the adaptive management of conservation. (FH)

Giant otter reproductive biology is still poorly understood and further studies into the mechanisms of reproductive suppression, delayed implantation, and pseudo pregnancy would greatly enhance our interpretation of observations in the field. It would also be helpful to learn more about fish population dynamics, fish abundance, and their breeding behaviour and migration patterns in order to understand fully the selective pressures acting on the giant otter. Do giant otters and caiman compete indirectly for fish? And what influence do giant otters have on fish populations? Can the giant otter be considered a keystone species — that is, one which plays a unique and crucial role in the way an ecosystem functions — such that if it were absent that ecosystem would change drastically?

To my knowledge, no study has as yet been carried out to quantify damage to fishing equipment caused by otters. And are fishermen justified in blaming otters for reduced fish catches or should they look closer to home for the explanation for overexploited fish stocks? Is the growing fish farm industry a potential source of future conflict? More detailed studies on the level, if any, of competition for fish between giant otters and subsistence, commercial, and sport fisheries are vital. And with artisanal gold mining rife in many parts of the giant otter's distribution range, is mercury bioaccumulating in giant otters and their prey and affecting their health and survival?

Lastly, due to the logistical difficulty and high cost of physically surveying aquatic habitats and establishing the limits of known species distribution on a large scale, giant otter researchers should develop innovative and systematic methods and tools for monitoring population distributions, abundances, and trends, and for projecting population change over the next quarter of a century. Long-term research projects designed to detect the impact of climate change on the distribution of giant otter populations are also vital.

CONSERVATION MEASURES

Giant otters exploit only a very small proportion of the rainforest or wetland habitat available, namely the riparian zone of a river, creek or lake, as well as adjacent swamps and water bodies. Any anthropogenic disturbance in this small area, and particularly those affecting otter territories and fish stocks therein, is likely to have disproportionate negative impacts on resident otter groups. Rivers are often the only means of access and transport for people, and communities and tourism operations are usually established on shorelines. Where once giant otters were persecuted to near oblivion for the pelt trade, now the species must contend with habitat destruction and degradation on a grand scale. How can we ensure that giant otter populations will survive this new onslaught?

The persistence of otter populations has been shown to be strongly influenced by the ability of dispersing individuals to move through the landscape. Giant otter conservation can therefore not just be about saving the otters; we must contribute to maintaining the integrity of entire watersheds, including headwaters and lowland habitats, and associated riverine and floodplain forests. Resilience of freshwater ecosystems will be the key factor influencing giant otter abundance and distribution in the future in many parts of its range. It is crucial to ensure connectivity among giant otter populations and reduce fragmentation by establishing and maintaining riparian corridors between otter habitats, in addition to the creation and expansion of protected areas and adequate strengthening and zoning thereof. Interchange of individual otters between sub-populations is necessary if we are to lower the probability of immediate risk of local extinction in the face of future threats.

Translocation and reintroduction of giant otters from areas where their populations now appear stable to areas where they are extinct or where their numbers are extremely low are currently being considered. One such project was started in 2007 in the Iberá basin in Argentina, where 150,000 hectares of private lands were purchased by The Conservation Land Trust to create a National Park. So far, populations of giant anteater, pampas deer, tapir, collared peccary, and green-winged macaw have been reintroduced, and jaguars are being bred on site for future reintroductions. In 2018, a pilot project aimed at reintroducing the giant otter into Iberá was drafted and presented to authorities for its approval, with the aims of restoring the ecological role of giant otters as top predators in the wetland ecosystem, while promoting their role as an ecotourism attraction for local communities. First releases will likely use captive individuals donated by international zoos, and further reinforcement with animals translocated from wild populations will be evaluated. If successful, this reintroduction will help restore the presence of the giant otter at the southern limit of its historical range. Projects such as this provide valuable insights for future restoration of the species in other regions, but require cautious planning and implementation, prioritizing considerations of habitat suitability, long-term population viability, and long-term financial and organizational commitment, and are not a substitute for protecting existing populations.

Developing effective mitigation strategies for human/otter conflicts is necessary to prevent killings of otter groups by local communities in retaliation for perceived or real losses. Mitigation measures could include not placing nets so that they block entrances or mouths of lakes and streams. Fisheries concessions and/or licences should also be explored as a management tool to reduce unsustainable fishing practices. A dialogue with communities and fishermen is necessary to determine how attitudes to giant otters might affect their conservation. Efforts to conserve fish resources in Amazonia will likely depend on regulation of human exploitation rather than management of giant otter populations.

Giant otter populations are recovering in some areas of their distribution range while others are on the decline. What does the next quarter of a century hold in store for them? (JG)

That giant otters are endangered animals strictly protected by law is not common knowledge within the giant otter's distribution range. Nor are local people always aware of how and to what extent their activities may negatively impact wildlife and their habitats. To this end, environmental education and awareness-raising campaigns, adapted for and targeted at different audiences, have been shown to be effective instruments in the giant otter conservation tool kit. The giant otter can act as a flagship or ambassador species for their aquatic habitats and for tropical rainforests as a whole, for example, by creating a giant otter main character in a story, puppet show, or wildlife festival, and the species can be presented as the umbrella that protects less visible, less known, and less appealing wildlife of aquatic habitats. Social media can also play a role; the IUCN Otter Specialist Group has an active presence on Facebook, as does the Friends of the Giant Otter community, thus facilitating communication between otter specialists and enthusiasts.

The giant otter's habitats frequently overlap with the most popular tourist destinations. Their repertoire of behaviours, which include energetic group hunting, interactions with caimans, basking on logs, mutual grooming, and play, make the giant otter an especially rewarding animal to watch. The species is frequently mentioned in advertising materials, and features regularly on t-shirts and logos. Whereas poorly managed tourism represents a danger to giant otters, conscientious ecotourism can contribute to the conservation of this flagship species by raising awareness of the plight of their habitats – prompting changes in consumer behaviour – and thus helping to prevent their destruction. It can also significantly change attitudes among those who are likely to perceive and experience the costs of coexistence, such that local people become champions of giant otter conservation, as long as they recognise the direct and indirect links between otters and tourism. Local people should benefit directly from tourism activities, for example, in terms of increased custom for local products and crafts, employment by lodges, or partnership in tourism ventures. In areas where there is a long history of nature tourism, giant otters are regarded as a key attraction and local people overcome their prejudices and learn to value the species as one worth protecting. However, significant benefits of tourism – as well as changed attitudes to otters – are often only felt after many years of sustained effort, and it is important not to raise expectations unduly to avoid disillusionment. Tourism is also not the catch-all activity to resolve conflicts between giant otters and local people: many areas are simply too remote for tourism to be viable and there are numerous inherent difficulties in establishing a successful tourism business. Since, in general, people do not identify culturally with the giant otter on a scale or in ways that is potentially significant for the species, alternative measures to mitigate potential conflict will need to be developed in these areas.

Demand for gold has existed for millennia and is not likely to decrease in the future. The gold price continues to be high and looks set to go up further. Given the activity's economic importance, control and regulation of gold mining will be difficult and military targeting of individual operations inadequate, without the support of national restrictions on mercury imports. Other approaches such as fair trade gold, technological innovations including mercury capture systems, and miner environmental education, will need to be implemented together with environmental restoration initiatives.

The development of national research and conservation action plans for the species is a pressing priority, and is underway or has been completed in several countries such as Colombia, Bolivia, and Brazil. Research groups currently working with giant otters should be strengthened and communication among them enhanced through regular workshops and other means.

Spreading the benefits and costs

So far, most of the costs of conservation (mainly in terms of restricted access to natural resources) have been shouldered by the comparatively small local native and settler population, while the majority of benefits (global climate regulation, oxygen production, wildlife viewing, and wilderness experience opportunities) have accrued to the international community. Successful conservation in Amazonia, whether of an endangered species like the giant otter or of an entire ecosystem, will ultimately depend on the social and economic security of the people of the region. In this sense, and from ethical and pragmatic considerations, we must succeed in spreading both the benefits and the costs of maintaining biodiversity.

In order for people to have an incentive to conserve wildlife and manage land sustainably, they should be directly involved in decision making, as well as receive direct economic benefits from biodiversity. However, experience

For better or for worse, nature is in our hands. (FH)

around the world shows that biodiversity management should not only be focused on generating monetary returns. Carefully taking into account local beliefs, values, and cultural norms are equally, if not more, important. Within the central precept that people, like the environment, change constantly, biodiversity conservation must be adaptive and open to novel ways in order to secure the meaningful participation of local inhabitants. For local, and especially rural, populations to benefit sustainably from biodiversity will require careful, long-term investment in training and infrastructure. Co-management by local people and the responsible national authorities is part of the solution towards a positive future for giant otters.

AND FINALLY…

During the last fifty years there has been significant progress in giant otter conservation in Amazonia. It seems likely, however, that the next fifty years will be much more difficult. In the same way that South American governments and private enterprise have historically supported the development of the mining, energy, timber, and agriculture sectors, currently the pillars of the regional economy, it is now time for Amazonia's other great wealth, biodiversity, to be the focus of long-term investment. With an enormous task and limited funds, conservation must

(JMR)

be as efficient, interdisciplinary, and participative as possible if we are to succeed in safeguarding the Amazon and creating true alternatives to the development pressures described in Chapter Four. Within this process, the giant otter can be an asset for nature tourism, a tool for biodiversity management, and an ambassador for the conservation of aquatic habitats.

We are just one of millions of species that live on Earth. Conservation, in its broadest sense, is about man's struggle to coexist with the rest of nature. A central concept of this coexistence must be the acceptance that mankind will only prosper if we manage to share the planet's resources. What, after all, makes us any more special than the giants of the Amazon?

How You Can Help

Whatever our age, location, or income, we can all contribute meaningfully to giant otter conservation. Following are some suggestions for how you, too, can help.

AS A READER OF THIS BOOK

Though I may never see giant otters in the wild myself, I know my personal actions and choices indirectly affect them. I accept and take responsibility for this impact, and I resolve to do all I can to help. So I avoid buying hardwood furniture and gold jewellery, invest in proven green companies, reduce or eliminate my consumption of meat (especially beef), use public transport or purchase an electric car, cut down on international air travel, become a member of a conservation organisation active in the Amazon region, and take every opportunity that comes my way to protect and plant trees. I elect politicians who do the same, and find different ways of making my voice heard and my talents count. I recognise that human overpopulation is the single greatest threat to all nature, but also that we have the capacity to instigate great positive change.

(JG)

AS A SCHOOLCHILD

I care about giant otters and try to find out as much as I can about them. I share everything I learn with my family and teachers and I give talks about giant otters at school so my classmates can know about them too. I encourage my parents to support a nature conservation organisation that works in the Amazon.

AS A TOURIST

As a well-informed and understanding visitor, I am aware that my visit might have an impact on giant otters and I respect the regulations required to protect them. I do not consider these regulations to be unnecessary restrictions. I prefer to travel with one of the recommended eco-tour organisers. I value a good tour guide highly. I will inform my fellow travellers and my guide, if necessary, about regulations. I give donations to support research and conservation projects in the areas I visit.

AS A TOURIST GUIDE

I am educated and informed about tropical rainforests and wetlands and participate in tourist guide training workshops. My goal is to introduce visitors to the beauty and value of the rainforest's unique ecology. I also explain problems and threats. I point out the rules which apply to protected areas, and encourage my clients to follow these rules. I never pursue giant otters with my canoe, not even if asked by my tour group, nor do I try to attract giant otters or approach too close to their den. I respect refuge areas and prefer to watch them from a platform or tower in order not to disturb these rare animals.

AS A TOUR OPERATOR

I make sure all my guides are well trained and certified. I respect the regulations for protected areas and do not agree to special requests by my clients which violate the rules. I try to involve local people in my enterprise. My means of transportation are as environmentally compatible as possible. I make sure my tours do not leave any waste in the area and that all waste is brought back into town. When planning and conducting my tours, I stay in close contact with the area's scientists and park rangers. In this way, I can ensure great tours and nature protection at the same time. I support research projects by allowing scientists to stay at my lodges for free or at cost rate.

AS A PARK RANGER

I make sure everybody respects the laws. In the case of a violation, I undertake the necessary actions. I am well informed about giant otters, the threats they face, and their protection. I am aware of my responsibilities: the maintenance of this protected natural area and the education of others about sustainable development and conservation.

AS A PROTECTED AREA MANAGER

I am aware of all the regulations for the protected area for which I am responsible and take the necessary steps when visitors violate these rules. I revoke permits or implement the relevant fines or restrictions when appropriate. I am informed about the scientific projects being conducted in the area and support projects that contribute to the protection of fauna and flora. I regularly travel in the protected area in order to talk to the local people and to garner my own impressions about what should be done. I make sure the park rangers are well trained and value the advice of anthropologists and wildlife researchers. In order to learn from management experiences in other protected areas, I stay in touch with relevant international organisations.

AS A GIANT OTTER RESEARCHER

I carry out my work without causing any threat to the species. I conduct my research carefully and actively collaborate with my peers. I am also concerned for the species other scientists are studying. I regularly prepare progress reports informing local authorities about my project, and share my findings in academic publications as well as national and international popular media.

AS A REPRESENTATIVE OF A NATURE CONSERVATION ORGANISATION

I consider it my task to arouse and promote sympathy for nature conservation. Public education is an important conservation tool. I logistically and financially support research and conservation projects and keep in touch with protected area administration and scientists.

AS A POLITICIAN

I believe it is important to receive information from a variety of organisations. I consider scientists, nature conservation organisations, regional administrations, but also the unions of farmers, land-owners, and gold miners to be my partners and allies. I am aware that existing protected areas are not sufficient to protect the giant otter's habitats. I try to create a tighter network of protected areas through new forms of protection, such as privately-owned reserves, indigenous peoples' reserves, or conservation corridors.

AS AN INHABITANT OF THE AMAZON

I am aware that fishing with monofilament nets, dynamite, or poison will destroy fish stocks, an important food source for me, my children, and giant otters. I realise, too, that gold mining and logging are very destructive. I also understand that giant otters do not significantly reduce my catch, that they belong here and are endangered, that they are indicators of a healthy ecosystem, and that I can potentially benefit from their presence. I do not kill them or chase them away.

The Giant Otter in a Nutshell

NAME

English:	Giant otter
Spanish:	Lobo de río, perro de agua, or nutria gigante
Portuguese:	Ariranha or arirai
Scientific:	*Pteronura brasiliensis*

TAXONOMY

Class:	Mammalia (mammals)
Order:	Carnivora (predators)
Family:	Mustelidae (mustelids)
Sub-family:	Lutrinae (otters)
Genus:	Pteronura
Species:	*Pteronura brasiliensis*

(ND)

SOUTH AMERICAN OTTER RELATIVES

Neotropical otter (*Lontra longicaudis*);
Marine otter (*Lontra felina*);
Southern river otter (*Lontra provocax*).

IDENTIFICATION

Total length:	1.5 – 1.8 m
Tail length:	53 - 70 cm, flat and broad, thick at the base.
Weight:	24 – 34 kg
Colour:	Body dark brown with an irregular, pale throat/chest marking, unique to each individual. The only otter species in which the nose pad, or rhinarium, is completely haired.
Form:	Long and low; hunched back; large, webbed feet.
Distinctive behaviours:	Periscoping and snorting, porpoising.

MISIDENTIFICATION

The sympatric Neotropical otter is often mistaken for a giant otter.

SEXING

Difficult to distinguish between males and females as similar in size. Gender only identifiable out of the water by observation of genitals or elongated teats.

AGE

Oldest documented life span for free ranging giant otters is 15 years, and 20 years in captivity. Cubs are between 0 and 6 months old, juveniles between 6 months and 1.5 years old, sub adults between 1.5 and 2.5 years old, and adults over 2.5 years old.

VOCALISATIONS

Highly vocal, communicating constantly with hums and coos. Snort at danger, and utter loud wavering screams in alarm or as contact call. Cubs can be heard begging at a distance of more than 500 metres.

DISTRIBUTION

Tropical lowland rainforests and wetlands in Venezuela, Colombia, Guyana, French Guiana, Surinam, Ecuador, Brazil, Bolivia, and Peru. Extremely rare in Paraguay. Extinct in Uruguay and Argentina. Never occurred in Chile.

HABITAT

Rivers, lakes, creeks, reservoirs, marshes, swamps, flooded forest. Aquatic habitats below 600 metres above sea level.

DIET

Almost exclusively fish, up to 4 kg per day.

FAMILIES

Live in groups of up to 16 individuals, but usually between 3 to 6. A group consists of a monogamous, breeding pair plus their offspring which may be adults as well as sub adults, juveniles, and cubs.

GESTATION

64 to 77 days

OFFSPRING

One litter per year, born during the dry season, 1 to 5 young are first carried out of the den at about one month old. At age 10 to 12 weeks cubs begin eating fish. They nurse until they are at least 5 months old. Cubs are cared for by the whole group.

DISPERSERS

Individuals, of either sex, who have attained sexual maturity and who have left their natal group. May form transient, non-breeding groups. Travel large distances in order to find a mate and an unoccupied home range to raise cubs.

ACTIVITY

Exclusively active during the day, group spends the night in a den or shelter. Hunting peak in early morning, between 7 and 9 am, and rest at midday. Often hunt again in the afternoon.

HOME RANGE

Small for a large predator, normally encompasses a variety of water bodies. Families may live in the same home range for many years.

COMPETITORS

Neotropical otter, caimans, piscivorous fish, and birds. Competition probably reduced by spatial separation, and differences in dietary preferences. Competition with humans is increasing.

NATURAL ENEMIES

Few natural enemies. Caimans are probably the most important. The anaconda and jaguar may also prey on giant otters. Otters may host skin and intestinal parasites, but the effect on mortality is unknown.

THREATS

Formerly hunting for the pelt trade, today habitat loss and fragmentation (due to deforestation and gold mining), over-fishing, water pollution, poorly managed tourism, domestic animal diseases (parvovirus and distemper), and occasional killing and taking of cubs to keep as pets.

STATUS

Categorised in the IUCN Red List as Endangered though some remnant populations are thought to be recovering. Total population size unknown.

PROTECTION

Listed since 1973 in Appendix I of CITES (Convention on International Trade in Endangered Species) which prohibits commercial international trade. Protected by law in all countries of its distribution range.

FURTHER RESEARCH NEEDED INTO

Ecology of dispersers and transient groups;
Population viability and genetics;
Natural factors of mortality;
Predator-prey relationships;
Conflict with people over fish;
Impact of gold mining and dams.

Author Biography

Jessica Groenendijk (JG) is a Dutch biologist and conservationist with a passion for connecting people with nature. Her work has been published in *BBC Wildlife Magazine*, *Africa Geographic*, *Earth Island Journal*, *The Island Review*, and *Zoomorphic*, amongst others. Her blog was Highly Commended in the International Category of the 2015 BBC Wildlife Blogger Awards and she is a Fellow of the International League of Conservation Writers. She was probably an otter in a previous life. Visit www.jessicagroenendijk.com or find her on Facebook, Twitter, and Instagram @ WildWordsAuthor

Contributing Photographer
Biographies

Frank Hajek (FH) is founder and Executive Director of Nature Services Peru, dedicated to creating shared value from nature's regenerative services (www.regenera.pe). Prior to this, Frank worked on the conservation of the giant otter in the Peruvian Amazon and then as national coordinator of Frankfurt Zoological Society programmes in Peru and later in Zambia. After two years as coordinator of the Ecosystem Services Working Group at the University of Oxford, Frank started Nature Services Peru (www.natureservicesperu.com) in 2009. Frank is a Director with B Corps Latinamerica and President of the non-profit Servicios Ecosistemicos Peru. He holds a master's degree in Engineering from Imperial College London, and an MBA from the University of Oxford.

Dr. Nicole Duplaix (ND) received her master's and doctorate degrees in Ecology from the University of Paris. Her doctoral research focused on the giant otters of Suriname, the first time this endangered species had been studied in the wild. She has studied otters and explored river systems worldwide for 45 years and is the founder and Chair of the IUCN/SSC Otter Specialist Group, the authority in global otter conservation. She co-founded TRAFFIC, the global wildlife trade monitoring network, in 1973, and set up TRAFFIC-USA. Nicole is a Senior Instructor at Oregon State University's Department of Fisheries and Wildlife and teaches courses in Conservation Biology and Species Recovery Planning. She is also a long-time contract photographer for the National Geographic Society.

Walter H. Wust (WW) is a forest engineer, journalist, editor, professional photographer, and analyst of environmental issues. With more than 30 years of experience and more than 500 published books, he is the editor of ecological and tourist topics with most experience in Peru. Walter is currently the director of Wust Ediciones, Guías Peru TOP, and WW Editores. He is also a Member of the Directive Council of the Peruvian Service for Protected Natural Areas (SERNANP), of the Technical Committee of the Peruvian Fund for Natural Protected Areas, and of the directory of the organisations EcoPesca, Instituto del Bien Común, and Líderes+1, as well as the company CCERO. Walter recently founded the Engineering and Environmental Management degree of the Peruvian University of Applied Sciences.

João Marcos Rosa (JMR) has a degree in journalism and specialises in documenting biodiversity and conservation in Brazil. His work has been published in numerous books and in magazines such as GEO, BBC Wildlife, and Discover and he has worked for the Brazilian edition of National Geographic since 2004. Rosa's photographs have been featured in the conservation campaigns of Greenpeace and UNESCO and he has received some of the most prestigious Brazilian awards, including Itau/BBA, New Holland Photojournalism, Avistar, and World Bird Photo Contest.

Dr. Ron Swaisgood (RS) serves San Diego Zoo Global as the Brown Endowed Director of Recovery Ecology. He also heads the Giant Panda Conservation Unit and is General Scientific Director of the Cocha Cashu Biological Station in Manu National Park, south-eastern Peru. Ron earned a bachelor's degree from the University of North Carolina at Chapel Hill and a PhD in Animal Behaviour from the University of California, Davis. He oversees conservation programmes for species as diverse as the California condor, desert tortoise, and Andean bear and has served as an adjunct professor at three universities. Ron is active on several international conservation committees, chairs the IUCN's Giant Panda Expert Team, and is past-chair for the Animal Behavior Society's Conservation Committee. He has also served on committees for the Children & Nature Network and San Diego Children & Nature Collaborative.

Dr. Fernando Trujillo (FT) is a marine biologist, with a masters in Environmental Science at the University of Greenwich) and a PhD in Zoology from the University of Aberdeen. He has recognised expertise in aquatic ecology with emphasis on aquatic vertebrates, endangered species, wildlife trafficking, wetlands inventory, and management and toxicology in aquatic ecosystems. Fernando is also Scientific Director of Foundation Omacha since 1993 and a member of the IUCN Cetacean and Otter Specialist Groups, with more than 200 published papers, action plans, books and books chapters. Last but not least, he is a keen wildlife photographer.

André Bärtschi (ABT) has a background in interior design from the Zurich School of Design and graphics studios. As a photographer he specializes in the natural history of tropical forests and spends part of the year in some of the remotest places of the New World tropics. His work has been published in renowned magazines such as GEO, BBC Wildlife, International Wildlife, Natural History, Smithsonian, and National Geographic, as well as in numerous nature books. Several of his photographs have won awards in the annual Wildlife Photographer of the Year Competition and, in 1992, he was awarded the top prize in this largest and most prestigious international contest of its kind.

Carlos Arévalo (CA) has a bachelor's degree in Education and a masters in psycho-pedagogy as well as more than 15 years of experience in the south-east of Peru in themes such as conservation, biodiversity, environmental education, climate change, and management of Protected areas. His work has focused on local people, indigenous communities, teachers, and government officials. His passion for conservation and education is his main motivation.

Dr. Adi Barocas (ABO) is a conservation biologist interested in carnivore behaviour and ecology. He serves as a postdoctoral associate with San Diego Zoo's Institute for Conservation Research and is currently leading a research project focused on the influence of gold mining activities on Peru's giant otter populations. Adi, who has also studied grey wolves in Israel and river otters in Alaska, has a love for the outdoors and spends a considerable proportion of his time in the field.

Bibliography and Further Reading

ANDERSON EP, JENKINS CN, HEILPERN S, MALDONADO-OCAMPO JA, Carvajal-Vallejos FM, Encalada AC, Rivadeneira JF, Hidalgo M, Cañas CM, Ortega H, Salcedo N, Maldonado M, Tedesco PA (2018) 'Fragmentation of Andes-to-Amazon connectivity by hydropower dams'. *Science Advances* 4: eaao1642

ANTUNES AP, FEWSTER RM, VENTICINQUE EM, PERES CA, LEVI T, Rohe F, Shepard Jr. GH (2016) 'Empty forest or empty rivers? A century of commercial hunting in Amazonia'. *Science Advances* 2: e1600936

BOUDOU A, MAURY-BRACHET R, COQUERY M, DURRIEU G, COSSA D (2005) 'Synergic effect of gold mining and damming on mercury contamination in fish'. *Environmental Science & Technology* 39(8): 2448-2454. doi: 10.1021/es049149r

BOZZETTI BF, CABRAL MMM, ROSAS FCW (2015) 'Cub biometry, litter size and reproductive period of giant otters (Pteronura brasiliensis) at the Balbina Hydroelectric Reservoir, Amazonas, Brazil'. *Latin American Journal of Aquatic Mammals* 10(2): 115-121. doi: 10.5597/lajam00203

BRACK-EGG, A (1978) 'Situación actual de las nutrias (Lutrinae, Mustelidae) en el Perú'. In: Duplaix N (Ed) Otters: Proceedings of the First Working Meeting of the Otter Specialist Group. IUCN, Morges, Switzerland. ISBN: 2-88032-200-6

BROSSE S, GRENOUILLET G, GEVREY M, KHAZRAIE K, TUDESQUE L (2011) 'Small-scale gold mining erodes fish assemblage structure in small neotropical streams. *Biodiversity Conservation*' 20:1013-1026. DOI 10.1007/s10531-011-0011-6

CABRAL MMM, ZUANON J, DE MATTOS GE, ROSAS FCW (2010) 'Feeding habits of giant otters *Pteronura brasiliensis* (Carnivora: Mustelidae) in the Balbina hydroelectric reservoir, Central Brazilian Amazon'. *Zoologia* 27(1): 47-53. doi: 10.1590/s1984-46702010000100008

CALAÇA AM, FAEDO OJ, DE MELO FR (2015) 'Hydroelectric Dams: The First Responses from Giant Otters to a Changing Environment'. *IUCN Otter Specialist Group Bulletin* 32(1): 48-58.

CARTER SK, ROSAS FCW (1997) 'Biology and conservation of the giant otter *Pteronura brasiliensis*'. *Mammal Review* 27: 1-26. doi: 10.1111/j.1365-2907.1997.tb00370.x

CARTER SK, ROSAS FCW, COOPER AB, CORDEIRO-DUARTE AC (1999) 'Consumption rate, food preferences and transit time of captive giant otters *Pteronura brasiliensis*: Implications for the study of wild populations'. *Aquatic Mammals* 25(2): 79-90.

CHEHEBAR C (1990) 'Action Plan for Latin American Otters'. In: Foster-Turley P, Macdonald S, Mason C (Eds). Otters: An Action Plan for their Conservation. Gland, Switzerland: IUCN/SSC Otter Specialist Group.

CORREDOR G, MUÑOZ NT (2006) 'Reproduction, behaviour and biology of the giant river otter Pteronura brasiliensis at Cali Zoo'. *International Zoo Yearbook 40*: 360-371. doi: 10.1111/j.1748-1090.2006.00360.x

DAVENPORT L (2008) 'Behavior and ecology of the giant otter (*Pteronura brasiliensis*) in oxbow lakes of the Manu Biosphere Reserve, Perú' [Doctoral dissertation]. Chapel Hill: University of North Carolina. 232 pp.

DAVENPORT L (2010) 'Aid to a declining matriarch in the giant otter (*Pteronura brasiliensis*)'. PLoS ONE 5(6): e11385. doi: 10.1371/journal.pone.0011385

DAVIDSON EA, DE ARAÚJO AC, ARTAXO P, BALCH JK, BROWN IF, BUSTAMANTE MMC, COE MT, DEFRIES RS, KELLER M, LONGO M, MUNGER JW, SCHROEDER W, SOARES-FILHO BS, SOUZA CM, WOFSY SC (2012). 'The Amazon basin in transition'. *Nature* 481(7381): 321-328. doi: 10.1038/nature10717

DEFLER T (1983) 'Associations of the giant river otter (*Pteronura brasiliensis*) with fresh-water dolphins (*Inia geoffrensis*)'. *Journal of Mammology* 64(4): 692.

DE OLIVEIRA GC, BARCELLOS JFM, LAZZARINI SM, ROSAS FCW (2011) 'Gross anatomy and histology of giant otter (*Pteronura brasiliensis*) and Neotropical otter (*Lontra longicaudis*) testes'. *Animal Biology* 61: 175–183. doi: 10.1163/157075511x566506

DE OLIVEIRA IAP, NORRIS D, MICHALSKI F (2015) 'Anthropogenic and seasonal determinants of giant otter sightings along waterways in the northern Brazilian Amazon'. *Mammalian Biology* 80: 39-46.

DIAS FONSECA FR, MALM O, WALDEMARIN HF (2005) 'Mercury levels in tissues of giant otters (*Pteronura brasiliensis*) from the Rio Negro, Pantanal, Brazil'. *Environmental Research* 98: 368-371.

DIRINGER SE, FEINGOLD BJ, ORTIZ EJ, GALLIS JA, ARAÚJO-FLORES JM, BERKY A, PAN WKY, HSU-KIM H (2015) 'River transport of mercury from artisanal and small-scale gold mining and risks for dietary mercury exposure in Madre de Dios, Peru'. *Environmental Science: Processes & Impacts* 17: 478-487. doi: 10.1039/C4EM00567H

DUPLAIX N (1980) 'Observations on the ecology and behaviour of the giant river otter (*Pteronura brasiliensis*) in Suriname'. *Revue d'Ecologie (la Terre et la Vie)* 34: 496–620.

DUPLAIX N, EVANGELISTA E, ROSAS FCW (2015) 'Advances in the study of giant otter (*Pteronura brasiliensis*) ecology, behavior, and conservation: a review'. *Latin American Journal of Aquatic Mammals* 10(2):179-202.

DURRIEU G, MAURY-BRACHET R, BOUDOU A (2005) 'Goldmining and mercury contamination of the piscivorous fish *Hoplias aimara* in French Guiana (Amazon basin)'. *Ecotoxicology and Environmental Safety* 60(3):315-323.

EVANGELISTA E (2004) 'Change of partners in a giant otter alpha couple'. *IUCN Otter Specialist Group Bulletin* 21(1): 47-51.

EVANGELISTA E, ROSAS FCW (2011a) 'Breeding behavior of giant otter (Pteronura brasiliensis) in the Xixuaú Reserve, Roraima, Brazil'. *IUCN Otter Specialist Group Bulletin* 28(A): 5-10.

EVANGELISTA E, ROSAS FCW (2011b) 'The home range and movements of giant otters (Pteronura brasiliensis) in the Xixuaú Reserve, Roraima, Brazil'. *IUCN Otter Specialist Group Bulletin* 28(A): 31-37.

FINER M, JENKINS CN, PIMM SL, KEANE B, ROSS C (2008) 'Oil and gas projects in the Western Amazon: Threats to Wilderness, Biodiversity, and Indigenous Peoples'. *PLoS ONE* 3(8): e2932. doi: 10.1371/journal.pone.0002932

GÓMEZ JR, JORGENSON JP (1999) 'An overview of the giant otter-fisherman problem in the Orinoco Basin of Colombia'. *IUCN Otter Specialist Group Bulletin* 16(2): 90-96.

GROENENDIJK J (1998) 'A review of the distribution and conservation status of the giant otter (*Pteronura brasiliensis*), with special emphasis on the Guayana Shield Region'. Netherlands Committee for IUCN, Amsterdam, 55 pp.

GROENENDIJK J, HAJEK F, DUPLAIX N, REUTHER C, VAN DAMME P, *et al.* (2005) 'Surveying and monitoring distribution and population trends of the giant otter (Pteronura brasiliensis) – guidelines for a standardization of survey methods as recommended by the giant otter section of the IUCN/SSC Otter Specialist Group'. *Habitat* 16. 100 pp.

GROENENDIJK J, HAJEK F (2006) 'Giants of the Madre de Dios'. Lima: *Ayuda para Vida Silvestre Amenazada-Sociedad Zoológica de Francfort Perú.* 160 pp.

GROENENDIJK J, HAJEK F, JOHNSON PJ, MACDONALD DW, CALVIMONTES J, STAIB E, SCHENCK C (2014) 'Demography of the Giant Otter (*Pteronura brasiliensis*) in Manu National Park, South-Eastern Peru: Implications for Conservation'. *PLoS ONE,* 9(8), e106202.

GROENENDIJK J, DUPLAIX N, MARMONTEL M, VAN DAMME P, SCHENCK C (2015a) '*Pteronura brasiliensis*'. *The IUCN Red List of Threatened Species 2015:* e.T18711A21938411. doi: 10.2305/IUCN.UK.2015-2.RLTS.T18711A21938411.en

GROENENDIJK J, HAJEK F (2015b) 'A reliable method for sexing giant otters in the wild'. *Latin American Journal of Aquatic Mammals* 10(2): 163-165. doi: 10.5597/lajamoo211

GROENENDIJK J, HAJEK F, SCHENCK C, STAIB E, JOHNSON PJ, MACDONALD DW (2015c) 'Effects of territory size on the reproductive success and social system of the giant otter, south-eastern Peru'. *Journal of Zoology* 296: 153-160. doi:10.1111/jzo.12231

GROENENDIJK J, HAJEK F, JOHNSON PJ, MACDONALD DW (2017) 'Giant otters: using knowledge of life history for conservation'. In: Macdonald DW, Newman C, Harrington (Eds) *Biology and Conservation of Musteloids.* Oxford University Press, ISBN: 9780198759805.

GUTLEB A, SCHENCK C, STAIB E (1997) 'Giant otter (*Pteronura brasiliensis*) at risk? Total mercury and methylmercury levels in fish and otter scats, Peru'. *Ambio* 26: 511–514.

HAGENBECK C, WÜNNEMANN K (1992) 'Breeding the giant otter *Pteronura brasiliensis* at Carl Hagenbecks Tierpark'. *International Zoo Yearbook* 31: 240-245.

HAJEK F, GROENENDIJK J, SCHENCK C, STAIB E (2005) 'Population census methodology guidelines for the giant otter (PCMG-GO)'. *Habitat* 16: 48-56.

HAJEK F, GROENENDIJK J (2004) 'Manejo de Cochas en el Parque Nacional del Manu, en base al Monitoreo de una Especie Indicadora'. Frankfurt Zoological Society.

HANTKE G, KITCHENER AC (2015) 'How to sex giant otter Pteronura brasiliensis (Gmelin, 1788) cubs'. *International Zoo Yearbook* 49: 214-218. doi: 10.1111/izy.12086

HENDERSON PA, CRAMPTON WGR (1997) 'A comparison of fish diversity and abundance between nutrient-rich and nutrient-poor lakes in the Upper Amazon'. *Journal of Tropical Ecology* 13: 175–198. doi: 10.1017/s0266467400010403

KIRKBY CA, GIUDICE-GRANADOS R, DAY B, TURNER K, VELARDE-ANDRADE LM, et al. (2010) 'The Market Triumph of Ecotourism: An Economic Investigation of the Private and Social Benefits of Competing Land Uses in the Peruvian Amazon'. *PLoS ONE* 5(9): e13015. doi:10.1371/journal.pone.0013015

KUHN RA, MEYER W (2010) 'Comparative hair structure in the Lutrinae (Carnivora: Mustelidae)'. *Mammalia* 74: 291-303. doi: 10.1515/MAMM.2010.039

LAIDLER K, LAIDLER E (1983) *The River Wolf*. Allen & Unwin. ISBN: 0-04-599008-5.

LAIDLER PE (1984) The behavioural ecology of the giant otter in Guyana [Doctoral dissertation]. Cambridge: University of Cambridge. 319 pp.

LEUCHTENBERGER C, MOURÃO G (2009) 'Scent-marking of giant otter in the southern Pantanal, Brazil'. *Ethology* 115: 210-216.

LEUCHTENBERGER C, ZUCCO CA, MAGNUSSON W, MOURÃO G (2014) 'Activity patterns of giant otters recorded by telemetry and camera traps'. *Ethology Ecology & Evolution* 26(1): 19-28. doi: 10.1080/03949370.2013.821673

LEUCHTENBERGER C, MAGNUSSON WE, MOURÃO G (2015) 'Territoriality of giant otter groups in an area with seasonal flooding'. *PLoS ONE* 10(5): e0126073. doi: 10.1371/journal.pone.0126073

LEUCHTENBERGER C, ALMEIDA SB, ANDRIOLO A, CRAWSHAW Jr PG (2016)' Jaguar mobbing by giant otter groups'. *acta ethologica* 19(2): 143-146. doi: 10.1007/s10211-016-0233-4

LIMA DDS, MARMONTEL M (2011) 'Return to the wild and reintegration of a giant river otter (*Pteronura brasiliensis*) cub to its family group in Amanã Sustainable Development Reserve, Brazilian Amazon'. *Latin American Journal of Aquatic Mammals* 9(2): 164-167. doi: 10.5597/lajam00183

LIMA DdS, MARMONTEL M, BERNARD E (2012) 'Site and refuge use by giant river otters (*Pteronura brasiliensis*) in the western Brazilian Amazonia'. *Journal of Natural History* 46(11/12): 729-739. doi: 10.1080/00222933.2011.654280

LONDOÑO GC, MUÑOZ NT (2006) 'Reproduction, behaviour and biology of the giant river otter *Pteronura brasiliensis* at Cali Zoo'. *International Zoo Yearbook* 40: 360-371.

MALHI Y, ROBERTS JT, BETTS RA, KILLEEN TJ, LI W, NOBRE CA (2008) 'Climate change, deforestation, and the fate of the Amazon'. *Science* 319: 169-172.

MCTURK D, SPELMAN L (2005) 'Hand-rearing and rehabilitation of orphaned wild giant otters, *Pteronura brasiliensis*, on the Rupununi River, Guyana, South America'. *Zoo Biology* 24: 153-167.

MENDOZA JA, HUAMANI K, SEBASTIAN G, OCHOA JA (2017) 'Distribución y estado poblacional del lobo de rio (Pteronura brasiliensis) en la cuenca del rio Madre de Dios, sureste del Perú'. *Revista Peruana de Biología* 24(2): 155-162.

MICHALSKI F, CONCEIÇÃO PC, AMADOR JA, LAUFER J, NORRIS D (2012) 'Local perceptions and implications for giant otter (*Pteronura brasiliensis*) conservation around protected areas in the eastern Brazilian Amazon'. *IUCN Otter Specialist Group Bulletin* 29(1): 1-67.

Ministerio de Comercio Exterior y Turismo, Peru https://www.mincetur.gob.pe/turismo/reportes-estadisticos-de-turismo/ (

MOURÃO G, CARVALHO L (2001) 'Cannibalism among giant otters (*Pteronura brasiliensis*)'. *Mammalia* 65(2): 225-227.

MUANIS MC, OLIVEIRA LFB (2011) 'Habitat use and food niche overlap by Neotropical otter, Lontra longicaudis, and giant otter, Pteronura brasiliensis, in the Pantanal wetland, Brazil'. *IUCN Otter Specialist Group Bulletin* 28A:76-85.

MUMM CAS, KNÖRNSCHILD M (2017). 'Territorial choruses of giant otter groups (*Pteronura brasiliensis*) encode information on group identity'. *PLoS ONE* 12(10): e0185733

NOONAN P, PROUT S, HAYSSEN V (2017) '*Pteronura brasiliensis* (Carnivora: Mustelidae)'. *Mammalian Species*, 49(953): 97-108.

NORRIS D, MICHALSKI F (2009) 'Are otters an effective flagship for the conservation of riparian corridors in an Amazon deforestation frontier?' *IUCN Otter Specialist Group Bulletin* 26(2): 73-77.

PALMEIRIM AF, PERES CA, ROSAS FCW (2014) 'Giant otter population responses to habitat expansion and degradation induced by a mega hydroelectric dam'. *Biological Conservation* 174: 30-38.

PICKLES RSA, GROOMBRIDGE JJ, ROJAS VDZ, VAN DAMME P, GOTTELLI D, ARIANI CV, IYENGAR A, JORDAN WC (2012) 'Genetic diversity and population structure in the endangered giant otter, *Pteronura brasiliensis*'. *Conservation Genetics* 13(1): 235-245.

PICKLES R, ZAMBRANA V, HOFFMAN-HEAP I, SALINAS A, GROOMBRIDGE J, VAN DAMME P (2011). 'An evaluation of the utility of camera traps in monitoring giant otter populations'. *IUCN Otter Specialist Group Bulletin* 28 (1): 39-45.

RAMALHEIRA CDS, BOZZETTI BF, DA CRUZ AD, PALMEIRIM AF, CABRAL MMM, ROSAS FCW (2015) 'First record of jaguar predation on giant otter (*Pteronura brasiliensis*)'. *Animal Biology* 65: 81-86.

RECHARTE M, BOWLER M, BODMER R (2008) 'Potential conflict between fishermen and giant otter (*Pteronura brasiliensis*) populations by fishermen in response to declining stocks of arowana fish (*Osteoglossum bicirrhosum*) in northeastern Peru'. *IUCN Otter Specialist Group Bulletin* 25: 89-93.

RECHARTE M, BODMER R (2009) 'Recovery of the endangered giant otter *Pteronura brasiliensis* on the Yavarí-Mirín and Yavarí Rivers: a success story for CITES'. *Oryx* 44: 83-88.

RECHARTE M, BRIDE IG, BOWLER M (2014) 'A recovering flagship: giant otters, communities and tourism in northern Peru'. *Wildlife Research* 41: 490-498.

RHEINGANTZ ML, SANTIAGO-PLATA VM, TRINCA CS (2017) 'The Neotropical otter *Lontra longicaudis*: a comprehensive update on the current knowledge and conservation status of this semiaquatic carnivore'. *Mammal Review* 47: 291-305. doi:10.1111/mam.12098

RIBAS C, MOURÃO G (2004) 'Intraspecific agonism between giant otter groups'. *IUCN Otter Specialist Group Bulletin* 21(2): 89-93.

RIBAS C, DAMASCENO G, MAGNUSSON W, LEUCHTENBERGER C, MOURÃO G (2012) 'Giant otters feeding on caiman: evidence for an expanded trophic niche of recovering populations'. *Studies on Neotropical Fauna and Environment* 47(1): 19-23.

RIBAS C, CUNHA HA, DAMASCENO G, MAGNUSSON WE, SOLÉ-CAVA A, MOURÃO (2015) 'More than meets the eye: kinship and social organization in giant otters (*Pteronura brasiliensis*)'. *Behav Ecol Sociobiol*. doi: 10.1007/s00265-015-2025-7

ROACH KA, JACOBSEN NF, FIORELLO CV, STRONZA A, WINEMILLER KO (2013) 'Gold mining and mercury bioaccumulation in a floodplain lake and main channel of the Tambopata River, Perú'. *Journal of Environmental Protection* 4: 51-60.

ROSAS FCW, ZUANON JAS, CARTER SK (1999) 'Feeding ecology of the giant otter, *Pteronura brasiliensis*'. *BIOTROPICA* 31(3): 502–506. doi: 10.1111/j.1744-7429.1999.tb00393.x

ROSAS FCW, DE MATTOS GE (2003a) 'Notes on giant otter (Pteronura brasiliensis) behavior in the lake of the Balbina hydroelectric power station, Amazonas, Brazil'. *The Latin American Journal of Aquatic Mammals*, 2, 127.

ROSAS FCW, DE MATTOS GE (2003b) 'Natural deaths of giant otters (Pteronura brasiliensis) in Balbina Hydroelectric Lake, Amazonas, Brazil'. *IUCN Otter Specialist Group* 20(2): 62-64.

ROSAS FCW, DE MATTOS GE, CABRAL MMM (2007) 'The use of hydroelectric lakes by giant otters *Pteronura brasiliensis*: Balbina lake in central Amazonia, Brazil'. *Oryx* 41(4), 520-524. doi: 10.1017/S0030605307000512

ROSAS FCW, CABRAL MMM, DE MATTOS GE, SILVA RE (2009a) 'Parental and alloparental care of giant otters (*Pteronura brasiliensis*) (Carnivora, Mustelidae) in Balbina hydroelectric lake, Amazonas, Brazil'. *Sociobiology* 54: 919–924. doi: 10.1017/s0030605307005121

ROSAS FCW, DA ROCHA CS, DE MATTOS GE, LAZZARINI SM (2009b) 'Body weight-length relationships in giant otters (*Pteronura brasiliensis*) (Carnivora, Mustelidae)'. *Brazilian Archives of Biology and Technology* 52(3): 587-591.

ROSAS FCW, RAMALHEIRA CS, BOZZETTI BF, PALMEIRIM AF, CRUZ AD, PATHEK DB, CABRAL MMM (2015) 'Sleeping sites used by giant otters (Pteronura brasiliensis) in the Balbina Hydroelectric Reservoir, central Brazilian Amazon'. *Aquatic Mammals* 41(2): 143-148. doi: 10.1578/AM.41.2.2015.143

ROSAS-RIBEIRO PF, ROSAS FCW, ZUANON J (2011) 'Conflict between fishermen and giant otters (*Pteronura brasiliensis*) in Western Brazilian Amazon'. *BIOTROPICA* 0: 1–8. doi: 10.1111/j.1744-7429.2011.00828.x

SCHENCK C, STAIB E, YASSERI AM (1995) 'Unterwasserlaute bei Riesenottern (*Pteronura brasiliensis*)'. *Zeitschrift fuer Saeugetierkd* 60:310-313.

SCHENCK C, STAIB E (1998) 'Status, habitat use and conservation of giant otter in Peru'. In: Dunstone N, Gorman M (Eds) *Behaviour and Ecology of Riparian Mammals*. Cambridge University Press, 359-370. ISBN: 978-0-521-63101-3.

SCHENCK C (1999) Presencia, uso del habitat y proteccion del lobo de rio (*Pteronura brasiliensis*) en el Peru. [Spanish translation of German doctoral dissertation]. Lima: Ludwig-Maximilians-Universitat, Munchen.

SCHENCK C, STAIB E (2001) 'Giant otter tourism in Peru: boom or bust for conservation'. In: Shackley M (Ed) Flagship species: case studies in wildlife tourism management. *The International Ecotourism Society*, 132 pp.

SCHENCK C, GROENENDIJK J, HAJEK F, STAIB E, FRANK K (2003) 'Giant otters in the Peruvian Rainforest: Linking Protected Area Conditions to Species Needs'. In: Bissonette J, Storch I (Eds) *Landscape Ecology and Resource Management*. Island Press, 341-357. ISBN: 1-55963-972-5.

SMITH NJH (1981) 'Caimans, capybaras, otters, manatees, and man in Amazonia'. *Biological Conservation*, 19, 177-187.

STAIB E (2005) Eco-Etología del Lobo de Río (*Pteronura brasiliensis*) en el Sureste del Perú [Spanish translation of German doctoral dissertation]. Ayuda para Vida Silvestre Amenazada – Sociedad Zoológica de Francfort Perú. 195 pp.

SWENSON JJ, CARTER CE, DOME J-C, DELGADO CI (2011) 'Gold Mining in the Peruvian Amazon: Global Prices, Deforestation, and Mercury Imports'. *PLoS ONE* 6(4): e18875. doi: 10.1371/journal.pone.0018875

SYKES-GATZ S, GATZ V (2011). *International Studbook for the Giant Otter (Pteronura brasiliensis). 2nd Edition.* Zoo Dortmund, Dortmund, Germany.

SYKES-GATZ S (2005) *International giant otter studbook husbandry and management information and guidelines. Husbandry and management of the giant otter (Pteronura brasiliensis), 2nd Edition.* Dortmund: Zoo Dortmund. 276 pp.

TOMAS WM, CAMILO AR, RIBAS C, LEUCHTENBERGER C, BORGES PAL, MOURÃO G, PELLEGRIN LA (2015) 'Distribution and conservation status of giant otter *Pteronura brasiliensis* in the Pantanal wetland, Brazil'. *Latin American Journal of Aquatic Mammals* 10(2): 107-114. doi: 10.5597/lajam00202

TREBBAU P (1978) 'Some observations on the mating behavior of the Brazilian giant otter (*Pteronura brasiliensis*)'. *Zoologische Garten* 48: 187-188.

UNPUBLISHED (2011) - National assessments evaluating the conservation status of giant otters in Suriname (Nicole Duplaix), Guyana (Zelda van der Waal), French Guiana (Benoit de Thoisy), Colombia (Fernando Trujillo, Juan Carlos Botello), Venezuela (Salvador Boher), Brazil (Danielle Lima, Miriam Marmontel), Bolivia (Veronica Zambrana, Rob Pickles, Pilar Becerra, Paul van Damme), Ecuador (Victor Utreras, Galo Zapata Rios), Peru (Jessica Groenendijk, Maribel Recharte, Rob Williams), Argentina (Guillermo Gil), Uruguay (Martin Buschiazzo), and Paraguay (José Cartes).

URYU Y, MALM O, THORNTON I, PAYNE I, CLEARY D (2001) 'Mercury contamination of fish and its implications for other wildlife of the Tapajós Basin, Brazilian Amazon'. *Conservation Biology* 15(2): 438-446. doi: 10.1046/j.1523-1739.2001.015002438.x

UTRERAS VB, SUAREZ ER, ZAPATA-RÍOS G, LASSO G, PINOS L (2005) 'Dry and rainy season estimations of giant otter, Pteronura brasiliensis, home range in the Yasuní National Park, Ecuador'. *Latin American Journal for Aquatic Mammals* 4(2): 191-194. doi: 10.5597/lajam00085

ZAMBONI T, DI MARTINO S, JIMÉNEZ-PÉREZ I (2017) 'A review of a multispecies reintroduction to restore a large ecosystem: The Iberá Rewilding Program (Argentina)'. *Perspectives in Ecology and Conservation* 15: 248-256. doi: 10.1016/j.pecon.2017.10.001

Index